A Celebration of the Movies—by John Lynch

. . .

More than 2100 birthdays listed for those
special people who have kept us
entertained since the early
days of Hollywood

. .

The **Hollywood**  TNT

Birthday

Book

With space
for listing your
own favorite birthdays
and other annual
occasions

.

Turner Publishing, Inc.

ATLANTA

Front cover: *Jean Harlow sparkles in the somewhat autobiographical role of Lola Burns—movie star—in* BOMBSHELL *(MGM, 1933).*

Back cover: *Clark Gable receives a telegram birthday cake (from his wife Ruth and agent Minna Wallis) on the set of* THE WHITE SISTER *(MGM, 1933).*

Frontispiece: *Joan Crawford celebrates her birthday with cast and crew on the set of* OUR DANCING DAUGHTERS *(MGM, 1928).*

Endsheets: *As Marguerite, Garbo celebrates her birthday in this lavish party scene from* CAMILLE *(MGM, 1937). Robert Taylor is at her right.*

Published by Turner Publishing, Inc.
A Subsidiary of Turner Broadcasting System, Inc.
One CNN Center, Box 105366
Atlanta, Georgia 30348-5366

FIRST EDITION
10 9 8 7 6 5 4 3 2 1

The Hollywood Birthday Book
Lynch, John
ISBN 1-878685-39-2

Distributed by Andrews and McMeel
A Universal Press Syndicate Company
4900 Main Street
Kansas City, Missouri 64112

Produced and Designed by John Lynch

Every reasonable effort has been made to
confirm all birth dates contained herein.
Errors formally pointed out to the publisher
will be corrected in future editions.

．　．　　．

For my own Glamour Girl
DIANE
"and her little dog too"

．　．

ACKNOWLEDGMENTS

For a small book, many thanks are in order to the
people at Turner Publishing who have helped with this
project: Woolsey Richard Ackerman, Robin Aigner, Crawford
Barnett, Kathy Buttler, Jane Lahr, Larry Larson,
Anne Murdoch, Walton Rawls, Michael Reagan,
Nancy Robins, and Michael Walsh.

．

Born on August 28th and 29th, respectively, Charles Boyer and Ingrid Bergman added the term gaslight *to the vernacular in the classic suspense drama by that name (*GASLIGHT, *MGM, 1944).*

Film noir *reached its pinnacle with the highly original society murder mystery* LAURA *(Twentieth Century-Fox, 1944), starring Clifton Webb and Gene Tierney. The pair were born November 19th and 20th.*

THE HOLLYWOOD BIRTHDAY BOOK is at once practical and entertaining. It provides ample writing space for each day of the year, so that you can list important birthdays, anniversaries, or other annual events. A glance each week, or even once a month, will keep you well informed of upcoming occasions.

There is something intriguing about sharing a birthday. It's fun to find out which famous Hollywood personalities were born on your own birthday or that of your friends—or even which stars were born on the same date. The combinations are often surprising, both in their similarities and diversities. One might not be surprised that Western legends John Wayne and James Arness, funny ladies Linda Lavin and Penny Marshall, or rock superstars Elvis Presley and David Bowie share birthdays. But who would have guessed that Louis Armstrong, Gina Lollobrigida, Neil Simon, Geraldo Rivera, Eva Marie Saint, and Louis B. Mayer were all born on the Fourth of July.

Among the more than twenty-one hundred celebrities listed are people who have kept us entertained since the beginnings of Hollywood. This is a collection of unforgettable personalities varied by type and era and in sufficient depth to delight the real movie devotee, yet it's broad enough to appeal to the average fan. Because the name Hollywood has come to represent the entire entertainment industry—not just feature films shot on California soundstages—among the stars included is a generous assortment of notables from television and foreign films as well. Also included are the birth dates of many moguls, producers, writers, directors, photographers, composers, designers, and media personalities who have lent their talents to creating the state of mind that is Hollywood.

INTRODUCTION

An average of six Hollywood celebrities are listed in the margin of each day's space. A complete *Index of Birthdays by Name* allows you to locate favorite stars within the listings, and also includes the *year* of birth for each.

Those interested in entertainment trivia will notice upon closer examination many *"birth date parallels"* throughout the year. Examples include:

■ Robert Duvall and Diane Keaton—who appeared together in THE GODFATHER and THE GODFATHER II—were both born on January 5th. The only two of Don Vito Corleone's children to survive into the third installment of this saga, Al Pacino and Talia Shire, were both born on April 25th.

■ Holly Hunter and William Hurt, cast as intense producer and vacant anchorman in the clever comedy BROADCAST NEWS, were both born on March 20th.

■ Jean Harlow is still remembered for her signature bias-cut evening dresses created for her by Hollywood's premiere designer Adrian—actress and designer were born on March 3rd.

■ Hoyt Axton and Bonnie Bedelia played father and daughter in the film biography of race car driver Shirley Muldowney, HEART LIKE A WHEEL—both were born on March 25th.

■ Forty years after Marlon Brando created a new acting style, portraying the brutishly sensual Stanley Kowalski in A STREETCAR NAMED DESIRE on Broadway, Alec Baldwin appeared in the same stage role. Both actors were born on April 3rd.

■ In the late thirties Alice Faye starred opposite Tyrone Power in a pair of diverting musical comedy-dramas: ALEXANDER'S RAGTIME BAND and ROSE OF WASHINGTON SQUARE. They share the birth date of May 5th.

Joan Bennett and Elizabeth Taylor played mother and daughter in FATHER OF THE BRIDE *(MGM, 1950) and its sequel,* FATHER'S LITTLE DIVIDEND *(MGM, 1951; pictured)—both were born on February 27th. The director of both films, Vincente Minnelli, was born on February 28th.*

During filming of WATERLOO BRIDGE *(MGM, 1940), director Mervyn LeRoy presents Vivien Leigh's birthday cake. Producer Sidney Franklin and co-star Robert Taylor look on.*

Facing page, top to bottom:

Flanked by Joan Crawford and Norma Shearer, director George Cukor (July 7) celebrates with a candle-studded watermelon (he was dieting) on the set of THE WOMEN *(MGM, 1939).*

Consummate character actress Marie Dressler (November 9) is shown on the occasion of her 62nd birthday with Gov. James Rolph (left) and Louis B. Mayer.

Liza Minnelli celebrates her 4th birthday (March 12) with father Vincente, holding a furry friend, and mother Judy Garland during filming of Judy's latest musical SUMMER STOCK *(MGM, 1950).*

- Stars of horror and mystery, Vincent Price and Christopher Lee appeared together in only one film, THE OBLONG BOX—both were born on May 27th. In the same "vein," Peter Cushing was born on May 26th.
- Composer George M. Cohan is listed in most reference books as having been born on July 4th; in reality he was born on the 3rd (his father had the date legally changed). Cohan's most famous song, "Yankee Doodle Dandy," contains the lyric, *"born on the 4th of July,"* which decades later became the title of a film starring Tom Cruise—also born on July 3rd.
- Oliver Stone directed Tommy Lee Jones as the villainous alleged conspirator Clay Shaw in the controversial JFK—actor and director were born on September 15th.
- In the roles of a highly religious Grand Rapid's businessman and a sleazy Los Angeles private detective, George C. Scott and Peter Boyle represented extremes in American culture in the hard-hitting HARDCORE. Both actors were born on October 18th.
- Brad Davis provided brief love interest for one of Sally Field's multiple personalities in the dramatic television miniseries SYBIL—both were born on November 6th.
- Maven and master of comedy, Bette Midler and Woody Allen teamed up as a couple celebrating their anniversary in SCENES FROM A MALL. Both stars were born on December 1st.
- Involved in the 1940s (a brief combination of romance and fisticuffs), eccentric film producer Howard Hughes and film beauty Ava Gardner were both born on Christmas Eve.
- Robert De Niro and Sean Penn appeared as convicts on the run in WE'RE NO ANGELS— they share the birth date August 17th.
- When William Frawley retired after five seasons of playing "Bub O'Casey" on television's

MY THREE SONS, his character was replaced by "Uncle Charley O'Casey" played by William Demarest. The two Williams were born on February 26th and 27th.

■ Born on August 16th and 17th, Madonna and Sean Penn shared the screen in the forgettable SHANGHAI SURPRISE as well as an explosive, if short-lived, marriage off-screen.

■ In many of her films Mae West was dressed by veteran designer Travis Banton. Among the costumes he created for her was the lion tamer's outfit she wore as Tira in I'M NO ANGEL—the only time Miss West *ever* appeared in pants. Actress and designer were born on August 17th and 18th.

■ Amy Irving's first two films (teen-revenge classic CARRIE and psychic chiller THE FURY) were directed by Brian De Palma. Actress and director were born on September 10th and 11th.

■ Kate Jackson and Harry Hamlin vied for the affections of Michael Ontkean in the frank but soft-spoken MAKING LOVE. The film's rival characters were born on October 29th and 30th.

■ In his last screen appearance Rock Hudson guest-starred on the nighttime soap, DYNASTY. He and his romantic foil for these episodes, Linda Evans, were born on November 17th and 18th.

Born on December 27th, Marlene Dietrich is reported to have been quite unhappy with the date. She said, "It's terrible—if I had been born a few days later I'd be a year younger." Following this rationale, one could speculate that the perfect birth date for the ever-glamorous Miss Dietrich would have been leap year's February 29th—she could then have been a mere quarter her age. Notables born during leap years include: Joss Ackland, Arthur Franz, Michèle Morgan, and William Wellman.

Facing page, clockwise from top:

Victor Fleming's birthday (February 23) is celebrated by cast and crew on the set of THE WIZARD OF OZ *(MGM, 1939)—notables include (left to right) Margaret Hamilton, Bobbie Koshay (Judy Garland's stand-in), Judy, Bert Lahr, Fleming, visitor Myrna Loy, Al Shenberg, and Frank Morgan.*

Twenty-three years after they filmed THE MERRY WIDOW *together, Jeanette MacDonald pays a birthday visit to Maurice Chevalier (September 12) on the set of* GIGI *(MGM, 1958).*

Eddie "Rochester" Anderson (September 18) reluctantly offers Mantan Moreland a birthday cigar on the set of CABIN IN THE SKY *(MGM, 1943).*

At right, top to bottom:

Here Louis B. Mayer joins Myrna Loy (August 2) and co-star William Powell for a piece of her cake on the set of ANOTHER THIN MAN *(MGM, 1939).*

During the filming of ZIEGFELD FOLLIES *(MGM, 1946) Lucille Ball (August 6) takes her birthday licks from a mustachioed Lionel Barrymore at her backyard "gay nineties" theme party.*

Lana Turner takes a break from shooting THE POSTMAN ALWAYS RINGS TWICE *(MGM, 1946) to help daughter Cheryl Crane (July 25) cut her second birthday cake.*

At a time when Oriental themes were the rage, most key roles were still acted by Occidental players. A glowing exception was Anna May Wong, who became an international star in films like SHANGHAI EXPRESS *(Paramount, 1932).*

January

1
DANA ANDREWS
CHARLES BICKFORD
VALENTINA CORTESA
XAVIER CUGAT
TY HARDIN
CAROL LANDIS

2
DABNEY COLEMAN
JULIUS LaROSA
ROGER MILLER
VERA ZORINA

3
VICTOR BORGA
MARION DAVIES
MEL GIBSON
ROBERT LOGGIA
RAY MILLAND
ZASU PITTS
ANNA MAY WONG

4 *Me me mine!*
WILLIAM BENDIX
DYAN CANNON
MATT FREWER
BARBARA RUSH
JANE WYMAN

5
JEAN-PIERRE AUMONT
ROBERT DUVALL
DIANE KEATON
PAMELA SUE MARTIN
MARIA SCHELL

In 1957 MGM produced the melodramatic musical
JAILHOUSE ROCK, *the story of a brooding convict turned brash rock 'n' roll star. Directed by Richard Thorpe and with a pulsating Lieber-Stoller score, it became the breakthrough vehicle for Elvis Presley.*

January

6

CAPUCINE
BONNIE FRANKLIN
SYLVIA SYMS
DANNY THOMAS
LORETTA YOUNG

7

NICHOLAS CAGE
VINCENT GARDENIA
TERRY MOORE
SHIRLEY ROSS

8

DAVID BOWIE
GRAHAM CHAPMAN
JOSÉ FERRER
BUTTERFLY McQUEEN
YVETTE MIMIEUX
ELVIS PRESLEY
SOUPY SALES

9

VILMA BANKY
FERNANDO LAMAS
HERBERT LOM
ANITA LOUISE
LEE VAN CLEEF
SUSANNAH YORK

10

RAY BOLGER
FRANCIS X. BUSHMAN
PAUL HENRIED
SAL MINEO

The near brittle surface of many of Faye Dunaway's characterizations has contributed to her "grande dame" persona. However, an ability to communicate the turmoil beneath has made her an outstanding actress, as in A PLACE FOR LOVERS (MGM, 1969).

January

11
LIONEL STANDER
ROD TAYLOR
GEORGE ZUCCO

12
KIRSTIE ALLEY
PATSY KELLY
KRESKIN
LOUISE RAINER
TEX RITTER
HENNY YOUNGMAN

13
KEVIN ANDERSON
KAY FRANCIS
OLIVER MESSEL
CHARLES NELSON REILLY
ROBERT STACK
RIP TAYLOR
GWEN VERDON

14
JASON BATEMAN
CECIL BEATON
BEBE DANIELS
FAYE DUNAWAY
JOSEPH LOSEY
CATERINA VALENTE
CARL WEATHERS

15
LLOYD BRIDGES
CHARO
CHAD LOWE
ANDREA MARTIN
IVOR NOVELLO
MARGARET O'BRIEN

Quintessential leading man Cary Grant joins Katharine Hepburn in a search for a dinosaur bone, as well as a tiger named Baby, in the relentlessly funny screwball comedy BRINGING UP BABY *(RKO, 1938).*

January

16

DEBBIE ALLEN
RALPH INCE
ALEXANDER KNOX
ETHEL MERMAN
DIANA WYNARD

17

JAMES EARL JONES
SHEREE NORTH
MACK SENNETT
BETTY WHITE

18

KEVIN COSTNER
CARY GRANT
OLIVER HARDY
DANNY KAYE
CONSTANCE MOORE

19 TAMARA · MICHELS

DESI ARNAZ, JR.
SHELLEY FABARES
GUY MADISON
DOLLY PARTON
NATASHA RAMBOVA
JEAN STAPLETON
FRITZ WEAVER

20

GEORGE BURNS
COLIN CLIVE
FEDERICO FELLINI
DEFOREST KELLEY
LORENZO LAMAS
PATRICIA NEAL
DOROTHY PROVINE

Ann Sothern moved easily from Broadway to film to television. She is shown here at her most glamorous in a George Hurrell portrait for BROTHER ORCHID (Warner Bros., 1940).

21

ROBBY BENSON
GEENA DAVIS
BENNY HILL
STEVE REEVES
TELLY SAVALAS
PAUL SCOFIELD
ANN WEDGEWORTH

22 ♥♥Hilarys B·day ⭐♥·· 1969

LINDA BLAIR
CONSTANCE COLLIER
D. W. GRIFFITH
JOHN HURT
PIPER LAURIE
CHRIS LEMMON
ANN SOTHERN

23

HUMPHREY BOGART
DAN DURYEA
SERGEI EISENSTEIN
RUTGER HAUER
ERNIE KOVACS
JEAN MOREAU
RANDOLPH SCOTT

24

JOHN BELUSHI
ERNEST BORGNINE
NASTASSJA KINSKI
MICHAEL ONTKEAN
ANN TODD
ESTELLE WINWOOD

25 ERINS B-DAY 1974

MILDRED DUNNOCK
DEAN JONES
DIANAH MANOFF
SOMERSET MAUGHAM
LEIGH TAYLOR-YOUNG

Tennessee Williams's bitterly poetic SWEET BIRD OF YOUTH *(MGM, 1962) told the story of a has-been film actress and her young lover. Geraldine Page and Paul Newman (pictured), Rip Torn, and Madeleine Sherwood recreated their stage roles.*

January

26
SCOTT GLENN
WILLIAM HOPPER
ANNE JEFFREYS
EARTHA KITT
PAUL NEWMAN
MOIRA SHEARER
ROGER VADIM

27
MIKHAIL BARYSHNIKOV
JOYCE COMPTON
TROY DONAHUE
BRIGETTE FONDA
DONNA REED
SABU
INGRID THULIN

28
ALAN ALDA
BARBI BENTON
ERNST LUBITSCH

29
W. C. FIELDS
JOHN FORSYTHE
ANN JILLIAN
KATHARINE ROSS
TOM SELLECK
MARC SINGER
OPRAH WINFREY

30
TAMMY GRIMES
GENE HACKMAN
JOHN IRELAND
DOROTHY MALONE
DICK MARTIN
VANESSA REDGRAVE
DAVID WAYNE

Tallulah Bankhead, remembered more for a tempestuous life-style off screen than for her performances on, is shown here, looking perfectly "daaahling," in FAITHLESS *(MGM, 1932).*

February

31 — JANUARY

TALLULAH BANKHEAD
EDDIE CANTOR
CAROL CHANNING
JAMES FRANCISCUS
SUZANNE PLESHETTE
JEAN SIMMONS
JESSICA WALTER

1

BIBI BESCH
JOHN FORD
CLARK GABLE
SHERMAN HEMSLEY
GARRETT MORRIS
STUART WHITMAN

2

CHRISTIE BRINKLEY
FARRAH FAWCETT
GALE GORDON
BONITA GRANVILLE
AYN RAND
LIZ SMITH

3

SHELLEY BERMAN
JOEY BISHOP
BLYTHE DANNER
MORGAN FAIRCHILD
STEPHEN McHATTIE

4

MICHAEL BECK
ROBERT COOTE
JAMES CRAIG
LISA EICHHORN
PAMELA FRANKLIN
IDA LUPINO

Moving from ash-blonde "sweater girl" to fully realized platinum leading lady in just a few short years, the elegant Lana Turner is shown here in one of her first memorable films, ZIEGFELD GIRL *(MGM, 1941).*

February

5
RED BUTTONS
JOHN CARRADINE
CHRISTOPHER GUEST
BARBARA HERSHEY
CHARLOTTE RAMPLING
DAVID SELBY

6
FABIAN
ZSA ZSA GABOR
PATRICK MACNEE
RONALD REAGAN
RIP TORN
ROBERT TOWNSEND
MAMIE VAN DOREN

7
EDDIE BRACKEN
OSCAR BRAND
DORA BRYAN
JOCK MAHONEY
JAMES SPADER

8
BROOKE ADAMS
JAMES DEAN
DAME EDITH EVANS
JACK LEMMON
AUDREY MEADOWS
NICK NOLTE
LANA TURNER

9
RONALD COLMAN
MIA FARROW
KATHRYN GRAYSON
GYPSY ROSE LEE
CARMEN MIRANDA
JOE PESCI
JANET SUZMAN

Along the way from teen-idol to confident leading man, Robert Wagner appeared in ALL THE FINE YOUNG CANNIBALS *(MGM, 1960): a tale of clashing relationships among a collection of rich and poor troubled youth.*

February

10

DAME JUDITH ANDERSON
KATHLEEN BELLER
LON CHANEY, JR.
LAURA DERN
JIMMY DURANTE
ROBERT WAGNER

11

EVA GABOR
TINA LOUISE
LESLIE NIELSON
BURT REYNOLDS
SIDNEY SHELDON
KIM STANLEY

12

JOE DON BAKER
CLIFF DEYOUNG
LORNE GREENE
ARSENIO HALL
JOANNA KEARNS
FORREST TUCKER
FRANCO ZEFFIRELLI

13

STOCKARD CHANNING
TENNESSEE ERNIE FORD
CAROL LYNLEY
DAVID NAUGHTON
KIM NOVAK
OLIVER REED
GEORGE SEGAL

14

JACK BENNY
FLORENCE HENDERSON
GREGORY HINES
THELMA RITTER
MEG TILLY
KEN WAHL

Like Johnny Weissmuller, Buster Crabbe was an Olympic swimming champion born to play Tarzan. As if for practice, Crabbe first appeared in the "Tarzan-look-alike" film KING OF THE JUNGLE *(Paramount, 1933).*

February

15
JOHN BARRYMORE
MARISA BERENSON
CLAIRE BLOOM
HARVEY KORMAN
CESAR ROMERO
JANE SEYMOUR
GALE SONDERGAARD

16
HUGH BEAUMONT
EDGAR BERGEN
SONNY BONO
LEVAR BURTON
WILLIAM KATT
CHESTER MORRIS
GRETCHEN WYLER

17 MONIQUES — ·
ALAN BATES
MARY BRIAN
BUSTER CRABBE
HAL HOLBROOK
LOU DIAMOND PHILLIPS
RAF VALLONE
VERA-ELLEN

18
EDWARD ARNOLD
MATT DILLON
ADOLPHE MENJOU
JACK PALANCE
MOLLY RINGWALD
CYBILL SHEPHERD
JOHN TRAVOLTA

19
JUSTINE BATEMAN
JOHN FRANKENHEIMER
SIR CEDRIC HARDWICK
LEE MARVIN
MERLE OBERON

Notorious for stealing scenes from even the biggest stars, Marjorie Main brought her irrepressible (often irascible) charm to every screen performance. At left, in MEET ME IN ST. LOUIS *(MGM, 1944).*

20

EDWARD ALBERT
ROBERT ALTMAN
AMANDA BLAKE
PATTY HEARST
JENNIFER O'NEILL
SIDNEY POITIER
PETER STRAUSS

21

CHRISTOPHER ATKINS
RICHARD BEYMER
TYNE DALY
GARY LOCKWOOD
RUE MCCLANAHAN
SAM PECKINPAH
ANN SHERIDAN

22 RUBY (CIRCE ✶ GRAHAM

DREW BARRYMORE
LOUIS BUÑUEL
ELLEN GREENE
GIULIETTA MASINA
JOHN MILLS
DON PARDO
ROBERT YOUNG

23

VICTOR FLEMING
PETER FONDA
JON HALL
DIANE VARSI

24

BARRY BOSTWICK
LINDA CRISTAL
STEVEN HILL
MARJORIE MAIN
EDWARD JAMES OLMOS
ZACHARY SCOTT
ABE VIGODA

Elizabeth Taylor; beauty, actress, author, pop icon, philanthropist, businesswoman —above all star—as "Maggie the Cat" in CAT ON A HOT TIN ROOF *(MGM, 1958).*

February

25

JIM BACKUS
DIANE BAKER
TOM COURTNEY
BRENDA JOYCE
ZEPPO MARX
WINIFRED "WINI" SHAW

26

GODFREY CAMBRIDGE
MADELEINE CARROLL
WILLIAM FRAWLEY
JACKIE GLEASON
BETTY HUTTON
MARGARET LEIGHTON
TONY RANDALL

27

JOAN BENNETT
WILLIAM DEMAREST
REGINALD GARDINER
IRWIN SHAW
ELIZABETH TAYLOR
FRANCHOT TONE
JOANNE WOODWARD

28

STEPHANIE BEECHAM
CHARLES DURNING
BEN HECHT
VINCENTE MINNELLI
ZERO MOSTEL
BERNADETTE PETERS
DOROTHY STRATTEN

1   MARCH

HARRY BELAFONTE
ROBERT CONRAD
ROGER DALTREY
RON HOWARD
DAVID NIVEN
DINAH SHORE

(See last page of the Introduction for celebrities born on leap year's February 29th)

Jean Harlow's platinum hair and curvaceous figure made her a super star in the thirties. A subtle talent for natural comedy, evident in roles like Lola Burns in BOMBSHELL *(MGM, 1933), made her a timeless legend.*

2

DESI ARNAZ, SR.
KAREN CARPENTER
JENNIFER JONES
BARBARA LUNA
LARAINE NEWMAN

3

ADRIAN
DIANA BARRYMORE
EDNA BEST
JEAN HARLOW

4

MARTHA O'DRISCOLL
JOHN GARFIELD
JOAN GREENWOOD
KAY LENZ
BARBARA MCNAIR
PAULA PRENTISS

5 GAYANNE

JACK CASSIDY
MYRNA DELL
SAMANTHA EGGAR
REX HARRISON
DEAN STOCKWELL

6

JAMES BRODERICK
LOU COSTELLO
ROCHELLE HUDSON
ED MCMAHON
ROB REINER

Exchanging dance for dialogue, the classic
NINOTCHKA *was remade with the scintillating*
Cyd Charisse as the gloomy Communist emissary
transformed by Paris and her first pair of
SILKSTOCKINGS *(MGM, 1957).*

March

7

JOHN HEARD
ANNA MAGNANI
PHILIP TERRY
DANIEL J. TRAVANTI

8

LOUISE BEAVERS
CYD CHARISSE
SUSAN CLARK
SAM JAFFE
AIDAN QUINN
LYNN REDGRAVE
CLAIRE TREVOR

9

CARL BETZ
TAINA ELG
RAUL JULIA
IRENE PAPAS
MICKEY SPILLANE
TRISH VAN DEVERE
JOYCE VAN PATTEN

10

WARNER ANDERSON
BARRY FITZGERALD
JASMINE GUY
KATHERINE HOUGHTON
CHUCK NORRIS
SHANNON TWEED

11 LISA WILKIE - AMANDAS GOLFRIEND

SALVADOR DALI
BRIGITTE FOSSE
DOROTHY GISH
JESSE MATTHEWS
LAWRENCE WELK

*In the grandaddy of all backstage movie musicals,
42ND STREET (Warner Bros., 1933), George Brent played
opposite Ruby Keeler (pictured) and Bebe Daniels. His
other leading ladies of the 30s and 40s included Garbo,
Stanwyck, Loy, De Havilland and Davis.*

12

BARBARA FELDON
GORDON MACRAE
LIZA MINNELLI
HELEN PARRISH
W. "BUCKWHEAT" THOMAS
GOOGIE WITHERS

13 *CYNTHIA KENDALL*

HENRY HATHAWAY
GLENNE HEADLY
TESSIE O'SHEA
DEBORAH RAFFIN

14

MICHAEL CAINE
BILLY CRYSTAL
QUINCY JONES
RITA TUSHINGHAM

15

GEORGE BRENT
MACDONALD CAREY
DAVID CRONENBERG
JUDD HIRSCH
CRAIG WASSON

16

BERNARDO BERTOLUCCI
ERIK ESTRADA
ISABELLE HUPPERT
JERRY LEWIS
CONRAD NAGEL
KATE NELLIGAN

Forever fretting "Oh, dear!" over the twisting plots of many of the best light comedy films, Edward Everett Horton is also remembered for his supporting roles in several of the Astaire/Rogers musicals. At left, with Betty Grable, in The Gay Divorcee *(RKO, 1934).*

March

17
Nat "King" Cole
Lesley-Anne Down
Patrick Duffy
Bridgitte Helm
Rob Lowe
Mercedes McCambridge
Kurt Russell

18
Irene Cara
Kevin Dobson
Robert Donat
Brad Dourif
Peter Graves
Edward Everett Horton
Vanessa Williams

19
Ursula Andress
Glenn Close
Louis Hayward
Patrick McGoohan
Phyllis Newman
Kent Smith
Bruce Willis

20
Ted Bessell
Wendell Corey
William Hurt
Holly Hunter
Ozzie Nelson
Carl Reiner
Theresa Russell

21
Matthew Broderick
James Coco
Timothy Dalton
Russ Meyers
Gary Oldman

Whatever one believes about her child-rearing capabilities, Joan Crawford's amazing combination of beauty, determination, and talent cannot be denied. At left, in LETTY LYNTON *(MGM, 1932).*

March

22

KARL MALDEN
ROSS MARTIN
MATTHEW MODINE
WILLIAM SHATNER
M. EMMET WALSH

23

JOAN CRAWFORD
CEDRIC GIBBONS
ERIC IDLE
AKIRA KUROSAWA
AMANDA PLUMMER
UGO TOGNAZZI

24

R. "FATTY" ARBUCKLE
JOSEPH BARBERA
ROBERT CARRADINE
RICHARD CONTE
STEVE MCQUEEN

25

HOYT AXTON
BINNIE BARNES
BONNIE BEDELIA
ED BEGLEY, SR.
PAUL MICHAEL GLAZER
ELTON JOHN
SIMONE SIGNORET

---

26 B'DAY OF THE ONE WHO BIRTHED YOU!

ALAN ARKIN
JAMES CAAN
VICKI LAWRENCE
CHICO MARX
LEONARD NIMOY
DIANA ROSS
MARTIN SHORT

In ALL FALL DOWN *(MGM, 1962)* Warren Beatty *portrayed the pivotal character Berry Berry. The bravado of his careless ne'er-do-well exterior was an almost involuntary disguise for innate feelings of self-doubt and recrimination.*

27

DAVID JANSSEN
GLORIA SWANSON
MICHAEL YORK

28

FREDDIE BARTHOLOMEW
DIRK BOGARDE
CONCHATA FERRELL
KEN HOWARD
FRANK LOVEJOY
DAME FLORA ROBSON
DIANNE WIEST

29

PEARL BAILEY
WARNER BAXTER
BUD CORT
EILEEN HECKART
TERENCE HILL
CHRISTOPHER LAMBERT

30

JOHN ASTIN
WARREN BEATTY
TURHAN BEY
RICHARD DYSART
PETER MARSHALL
PAUL REISER
SHIRLEY STOLLER

31

RICHARD CHAMBERLAIN
SHIRLEY JONES
RICHARD KILEY
ED MARINARO
HENRY MORGAN
RHEA PEARLMAN
CHRISTOPHER WALKEN

Bette Davis, as fiercely independent in life as the characters she portrayed on film, became queen of the "woman's" movie in classic vehicles like Now Voyager *(Warner Bros., 1942)—shown here with Paul Henreid.*

April

1
WALLACE BEERY
LON CHANEY, SR.
GORDON JUMP
ALI MACGRAW
ANNETTE O'TOOLE
JANE POWELL
DEBBIE REYNOLDS

2
BUDDY EBSEN
RITA GAM
SIR ALEC GUINNESS
LINDA HUNT
PAMELA REED
JACK WEBB

3
ALEC BALDWIN
MARLON BRANDO
DORIS DAY
GEORGE JESSEL
EDDIE MURPHY
WAYNE NEWTON
JAN STERLING

4
BEA BENADERET
ROBERT DOWNEY, JR.
CHRISTINE LAHTI
FRANCES LANGFORD
CRAIG T. NELSON
MICHAEL PARKS

5
ROGER CORMAN
BETTE DAVIS
MELVYN DOUGLAS
CHRISTOPHER HEWETT
MICHAEL MORIARTY
GREGORY PECK
SPENCER TRACY

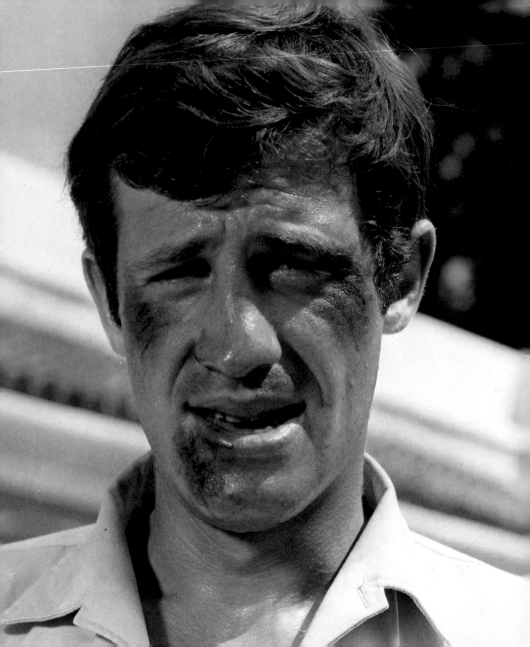

Often playing "the thoughtful tough," Jean-Paul Belmondo moved effortlessly from New Wave French to major international films such as GREED IN THE SUN (MGM, 1965). He is shown here in this desert action adventure's climactic fight sequence.

6

MARILU HENNER
WALTER HUSTON
MICHELLE PHILLIPS
JOHN RATZENBERGER
GEORGE REEVES
ROY THINNES
BILLY DEE WILLIAMS

7

FRANCIS FORD COPPOLA
DAVID FROST
JAMES GARNER
WAYNE ROGERS
WALTER WINCHELL

8

ILKA CHASE
JOHN GAVIN
SHECKY GREENE
SONJA HENIE
MARY PICKFORD
JOHN SCHNEIDER

9

JEAN-PAUL BELMONDO
WARD BOND
BRANDON DE WILDE
PAULINA PORIZKOVA
DENNIS QUAID
PAUL ROBESON

10 MARLA SARA SMITH (1 YR. OLDER THAN YOU! 2/M

GEORGE ARLISS
CHUCK CONNORS
DON MEREDITH
HARRY MORGAN
OMAR SHARIF
MAX VON SYDOW

MGM's celebrated Arthur Freed unit produced its own version of vaudeville in EASTER PARADE *(1948) with a musical triangle of stars comprised of Judy Garland, Fred Astaire, and the vivacious Texas beauty Ann Miller.*

11

PAUL DOUGLAS
JOEL GREY
LOUISE LASSER

12

DAVID CASSIDY
SHANNEN DOHERTY
ANDY GARCIA
DAVID LETTERMAN
ANN MILLER
ED O'NEIL
JANE WITHERS

13

DON ADAMS
TONY DOW
EDWARD FOX
HOWARD KEEL
SAUNDRA SANTIAGO
RICKY SCHRODER
LYLE WAGGONER

14

JULIE CHRISTIE
BRADFORD DILLMAN
SIR JOHN GIELGUD
LORETTA LYNN
ANTHONY PERKINS
ROD STEIGER
LEE TRACY

15

CLAUDIA CARDINALE
LITA GREY CHAPLIN
HANS CONRIED
ELIZABETH MONTGOMERY

From his first major screen role, that of Joe Bonaparte, prizefighter/violinist, in GOLDEN BOY (Columbia, 1939), William Holden was noted for his ability to make audiences feel they knew him—personally.

April

16
Edie Adams
Ellen Barkin
Sir Charles Chaplin
Jon Cryer
Fifi D'Orsay
Henry Mancini
Peter Ustinov

17
William Holden
Arthur Lake
Paul Langton
Thornton Wilder

18
Barbara Hale
Dorothy Lyman
Hayley Mills
Rick Moranis
Virginia O'Brien
Eric Roberts
James Woods

19
Tim Curry
Elinor Donahue
Jayne Mansfield
Dudley Moore
Hugh O'Brian
May Robson
Vivienne Segal

20
Bruce Cabot
Nina Foch
Jessica Lange
Harold Lloyd
Ryan O'Neal
George Takei
Elena Verdugo

Playing comedy with the subtle realism of a serious dramatic actress, and drama with the off-beat warmth of a fine comedienne, Shirley MacLaine forged a unique career that completely meshes the two. At left, in Two Loves *(MGM, 1961).*

April

21
Tony Danza
Charles Grodin
Patti LuPone
Elaine May
Anthony Quinn

22
Eddie Albert
Joseph Bottoms
Glen Campbell
Jason Miller
Jack Nicholson
Charlotte Rae

23
Valerie Bertinelli
Janet Blair
Sandra Dee
Joyce DeWitt
Lee Majors
Shirley Temple

24
Leslie Howard
Jill Ireland
Shirley MacLaine
Barbra Streisand

25
Denny (Scott) Miller
Edward R. Murrow
Al Pacino
Talia Shire

Pan-Americana (1945) was an RKO version of the recurring slick musical comedy with a South American locale. The irreplaceable Eve Arden added her particular sparkle via the elegantly caustic wisecrack.

April

CAROL BURNETT
CHARLES K. FELDMAN
ANITA LOOS
CECILIA PARKER
BOBBY RYDELL
WILLIAM DESMOND TAYLOR

26

ANOUK AIMÉE
SANDY DENNIS
JACK KLUGMAN

27

ANN-MARGRET
LIONEL BARRYMORE
CAROLYN JONES
JAY LENO

28

DANIEL DAY LEWIS
TOM EWELL
CELESTE HOLM
KATE MULGREW
MICHELLE PFEIFFER
EVE PLUMB
UMA THURMAN

29

EVE ARDEN
CORINE CALVET
JILL CLAYBURGH
PERRY KING
CLORIS LEACHMAN

30

Audrey Hepburn, an original in personality and appearance, continued to bring a little bit of Cinderella to everything she did. Here, in the glittering Billy Wilder comedy SABRINA (Paramount, 1954).

May

1
DANIELLE DARRIEUX
GLENN FORD
JOAN HACKETT
LOUIS NYE
JACK PAAR
KATE SMITH

2
BRIAN AHERNE
ROSCOE LEE BROWN
BING CROSBY
BIANCA JAGGER
LORENZO MUSIC
JO ANN PFLUG
TYRONE POWER, SR.

3
MARY ASTOR
BEULAH BONDI
BETTY COMDEN
WALTER SLEZAK
EARL WILSON
GEORGE "FOGHORN" WINSLOW

4
HOWARD DA SILVA
AUDREY HEPBURN
TAMMY WYNETTE

5
ANN B. DAVIS
ALICE FAYE
WILL HUTCHINS
JUNE LANG
TYRONE POWER

Gary Cooper was a favorite of male and female moviegoers alike. His powerful quiet charm turned an extra into one of the best-known names in film history. At left, in OPERATOR 13 *(MGM, 1933).*

May

6

STEWART GRANGER
BEN MASTERS
MAX OPULS (OPHÜLS)
LORI SINGER
RUDOLPH VALENTINO
ORSON WELLES
MARE WINNINGHAM

7

ANNE BAXTER
GARY COOPER
GEORGE "GABBY" HAYES
DARREN MCGAVIN

8

LEX BARKER
MELISSA GILBERT
SALOME JENS
DAVID KEITH
RICK NELSON
DON RICKLES
ROBERTO ROSSELLINI

9

RICHARD BARTHELMESS
CANDICE BERGEN
ALBERT FINNEY
GLENDA JACKSON
MIKE WALLACE

10

FRED ASTAIRE
ANATOLE LITVAK
MARIE-FRANCE PISIER
DAVID O. SELZNICK
MAX STEINER
NANCY WALKER

James Mason built a career playing handsome, erudite leading men—often with a dark side just below the surface. He is shown here in the superior Hollywood all-star soaper EAST SIDE, WEST SIDE (MGM, 1949).

May

11

DOUG MCCLURE
NATASHA RICHARDSON
DAME MARGARET RUTHERFORD
PHIL SILVERS

12

BRUCE BOXLEITNER
GEORGE CARLIN
EMILIO ESTEVEZ
KATHARINE HEPBURN
WILFRED HYDE-WHITE

13

BEATRICE ARTHUR
SENTA BERGER
KAREN CELLINI
BUCK TAYLOR

14

FRANCESCA ANNIS
BOBBY DARIN
MEG FOSTER
SEASON HUBLEY
PATRICE MUNSEL

15

JOSEPH COTTEN
CONSTANCE CUMMINGS
LEE HORSLEY
LAINIE KAZAN
JAMES MASON

Before THE LADY EVE, *Henry Fonda (pictured) and Barbara Stanwyck put on their "mad caps" and combined talents for* THE MAD MISS MANTON *(RKO, 1938)—the story of a newspaper editor, seven dizzy debs, and a double murder.*

May

16
PIERCE BROSNAN
HENRY FONDA
JANET JACKSON
LIBERACE
TORI SPELLING
MARGARET SULLAVAN

17
RUTH DONNELLY
DENNIS HOPPER
BRIGITTE NIELSEN
MAUREEN O'SULLIVAN
DEBRA WINGER

18
FRANK CAPRA
PERRY COMO
DWAYNE HICKMAN
BILL MACY
ROBERT MORSE
PRISCILLA POINTER
PERNELL ROBERTS

19
BRUCE BENNETT
JAMES FOX
DAVID HARTMAN
GRACE JONES
NANCY KWAN
BEVERLY ROBERTS
ROBERT WILCOX

20
CHER
GEORGE GOBEL
BRONSON PINCHOT
LYDA ROBERTI
JAMES STEWART
DAVE THOMAS

As Mr. Darcy in Jane Austen's charmingly humorous
PRIDE AND PREJUDICE *(MGM, 1940), Laurence*
Olivier created a character rich in period manners,
but with a subtle underlying virility that helps set
this film apart from other period pieces.

May

21

RAYMOND BURR
PEGGY CASS
LOLA LANE
ROBERT MONTGOMERY
MR. T. (LAWRENCE TERO)

22

RICHARD BENJAMIN
FRANK CONVERSE
LORD LAURENCE OLIVIER
BARBARA PARKINS
MICHAEL SARRAZIN
SUSAN STRASBERG
PAUL WINFIELD

23

BARBARA BARRIE
ROSEMARY CLOONEY
JOAN COLLINS
DOUGLAS FAIRBANKS, SR.
BETTY GARRETT
HERBERT MARSHALL
JOHN PAYNE

24

GARY BURGHOFF
TOMMY CHONG
ELSA MAXWELL
SIOBHAN MCKENNA
LILLI PALMER
PRISCILLA PRESLEY

25

DIXIE CARTER
STEVE COCHRAN
JEAN CRAIN
ROBERT MORLEY
FRANK OZ
CONNIE SELLECCA
KAREN VALENTINE

Not only were his film characters larger than life, John Wayne himself, after 250 films, became inseparable from his image as the quintessential American hero of his era. Typical "Duke," FORT APACHE (RKO, 1948).

26

JAMES ARNESS
PETER CUSHING
PEGGY LEE
BILL "BOJANGLES" ROBINSON
JAY "TONTO" SILVERHEELS
JOHN WAYNE

27

LOUIS GOSSETT, JR.
DASHIELL HAMMETT
CHRISTOPHER LEE
LEE MERIWETHER
VINCENT PRICE
LUCILLE WATSON

28

CARROLL BAKER
BRANDON CRUZ
SONDRA LOCKE

29

IRIS ADRIAN
ANNETTE BENING
HELMUT BERGER
ANTHONY GEARY
BOB HOPE
BEATRICE LILLIE
JOSEF VON STERNBERG

30

MEL BLANC
KEIR DULLEA
JIMMY LYDON
L. T. "STEPIN FETCHIT" PERRY
MICHAEL J. POLLARD
IRVING THALBERG
CLINT WALKER

Naughty yet innocent, instinctively an actress, incandescently photogenic, and with the ability to expose her own reality through film characters, Marilyn Monroe became the most famous star in history. THE ASPHALT JUNGLE (MGM, 1950).

MAY

31

DON AMECHE
TOM BERENGER
CLINT EASTWOOD
SHARON GLESS
GREGORY HARRISON
JIM HUTTON
BROOKE SHIELDS

1

JOAN CAUFIELD
MORGAN FREEMAN
ANDY GRIFFITH
GEORGE HURRELL
CLEAVON LITTLE
MARILYN MONROE
EDWARD WOODWARD

2

HEDDA HOPPER
STACY KEACH
SALLY KELLERMAN
JERRY MATHERS
BUTCH PATRICK
JOHNNY WEISSMULLER

3

JOSEPHINE BAKER
CHUCK BARRIS
TONY CURTIS
COLLEEN DEWHURST
MAURICE EVANS
PAULETTE GODDARD

---

4 TY (GXYANNES)

BRUCE DERN
ALLA NAZIMOVA
ROSALIND RUSSELL
PARKER STEVENSON
DENNIS WEAVER
DR. RUTH WESTHEIMER

While developing into a sophisticated leading lady, exquisite Alexis Smith spent a decade as a contract player. Among her early films is the Jack Benny comedy-fantasy THE HORN BLOWS AT MIDNIGHT *(Warner Bros., 1945).*

June

WILLIAM BOYD
ROBERT LANSING
BILL MOYERS
WALTER PLUNKETT

5

SANDRA BERNHARD
DANA CARVEY
ROBERT ENGLUND
MARIA MONTEZ

6

DOLORES GRAY
JAMES IVORY
TOM JONES
VIRGINIA MCKENNA
KEN OSMOND
PRINCE
JESSICA TANDY

7

JAMES DARREN
GRIFFIN DUNNE
MILLICENT MARTIN
ROBERT PRESTON
JOAN RIVERS
ALEXIS SMITH
DANA WYNTER

8

GEORGE AXELROD
ROBERT CUMMINGS
JOHNNY DEPP
MICHAEL J. FOX
MONA FREEMAN
JACKIE MASON
COLE PORTER

9

Judy Garland's dedication in combination with great talent created a stage, screen, and recording superstar. The reality and warmth of her personality left behind a cult that extends beyond mere legend. At left in PRESENTING LILY MARS *(MGM, 1943).*

June

10

CLYDE BEATTY
JUDY GARLAND
HATTIE MCDANIEL
GARDNER MCKAY
SIR TERENCE RATTIGAN
ANDREW STEVENS

11

ADRIENNE BARBEAU
JANE BRYAN
CHAD EVERETT
RICHARD TODD
GENE WILDER

12

VIC DAMONE
PRISCILLA LANE
WILLIAM LUNDIGAN
JIM NABORS
VERA HRUBA RALSTON

13

RALPH EDWARDS
IAN HUNTER
PAUL LYNDE
BASIL RATHBONE
ALLY SHEEDY
RICHARD THOMAS

14

GENE BARRY
MARLA GIBBS
BURL IVES
DOROTHY MCGUIRE
WILL PATTON

The range of Louis Jourdan's talent is displayed in the role of the idealistic cynic Gaston Lachaille (at left with Leslie Caron) in the diverting musical version of a story by Collette, GIGI *(MGM, 1958).*

June

15

JAMES BELUSHI
JULIE HAGERTY
NEIL PATRICK HARRIS
HARRY LANGDON
AL "LASH" LA RUE
BELINDA LEE
DAVID ROSE

16

JACK ALBERTSON
FAITH DOMERGUE
STAN LAUREL
ILONA MASSEY
JOAN VAN ARK

17

RALPH BELLAMY
MARK LINN-BAKER
DEAN MARTIN
JOE PISCOPO
PHYLICIA RASHAD
BERYL REID

18

MARA HOBEL
CAROL KANE
JEANETTE MACDONALD
E. G. MARSHALL
ISABELLA ROSSELLINI
BLANCHE SWEET
LINDA THORSON

19

PIER ANGELI
LOUIS JOURDAN
MALCOLM MCDOWELL
MILDRED NATWICK
GENA ROWLANDS
KATHLEEN TURNER
DAME MAY WHITTY

A year after arriving in Hollywood, Errol Flynn became a star in CAPTAIN BLOOD *(Warner Bros., 1935). His greatest successes continued to lie in similar costume adventures that made him the archetypal romantic swashbuckler.*

20

DANNY AIELLO
CANDY CLARKE
ERROL FLYNN
JOHN GOODMAN
NICOLE KIDMAN
MARTIN LANDAU
CYNDI LAUPER

21

MEREDITH BAXTER
SAMI DAVIS
JOE FLAHERTY
MARIETTE HARTLEY
JUDY HOLLIDAY
JANE RUSSELL
MAUREEN STAPLETON

22

KLAUS MARIA BRANDAUER
TRACY POLLAN
FREDDIE PRINZE
MERYL STREEP
MIKE TODD
LINDSAY WAGNER
BILLY WILDER

23

BOB FOSSE
TED SHACKELFORD
IRENE WORTH

24

NANCY ALLEN
JACK CARTER
MICHELE LEE
PETER WELLER

In CAGED (Warner Bros., 1950) Eleanor Parker gave one of her most memorable performances as an innocent girl sent to prison where she becomes the woman she had previously only been accused of being.

June

GEORGE ABBOT
CHARLOTTE GREENWOOD
PETER LIND HAYES
JUNE LOCKHART
SIDNEY LUMET

25

PAMELA BELLWOOD
JEANNE EAGLES
PETER LORRE
ELEANOR PARKER
KATHY BATES

26

ISABELLE ADJANI
JULIA DUFFY
JOHN MCINTIRE
LORENZO "THE BLACK
    VALENTINO" TUCKER

27

MEL BROOKS
JOHN CUSACK
GILDA RADNER
LOIS WILSON

28

IAN BANNEN
GARY BUSEY
JOAN DAVIS
NELSON EDDY
KAY KENDALL
SLIM PICKENS
RUTH WARRICK

29

A unique combination of femininity and fire, Susan Hayward never gave less than her all to any role, especially not in her stand-out performance as Lillian Roth in I'LL CRY TOMORROW (MGM, 1955).

30

MADGE BELLAMY
SUSAN HAYWARD
LENA HORNE
BUDDY RICH

1

DAN ACKROYD
KAREN BLACK
GENEVIÈVE BUJOLD
LESLIE CARON
FARLEY GRANGER
OLIVIA DE HAVILLAND
CHARLES LAUGHTON

2

JERRY HALL
POLLY HOLLIDAY
ROBERT ITO
CHERYL LADD
DAN ROWAN
RON SILVER

3

BETTY BUCKLEY
GEORGE M. COHAN
TOM CRUISE
DOROTHY KILGALLEN
KEN RUSSELL
GEORGE SANDERS

4

LOUIS ARMSTRONG
GERTRUDE LAWRENCE
GINA LOLLOBRIGIDA
LOUIS B. MAYER
GERALDO RIVERA
EVA MARIE SAINT
NEIL SIMON

In films like the fast paced underworld drama Rogue Cop *(MGM, 1954) Janet Leigh began to move from strictly "girl next door" roles to the more sophisticated persona that would lead to* Psycho, A Touch of Evil, *and other memorable roles.*

5

Jean Cocteau
Katherine Helmond
Shirley Knight
Isa Miranda
Warren Oates

6

Ned Beatty
Fred Dryer
Merv Griffin
Janet Leigh
Nancy (Davis) Reagan
Della Reese
Sylvester Stallone

7

George Cukor
Vittorio De Sica
Shelley Duvall
Doc Severinsen

8

Kevin Bacon
Kim Darby
Marty Feldman
Anjelica Huston
Eugene Pallette
Craig Stevens

9

Brian Dennehy
Vince Edwards
Tom Hanks
Kelly McGillis
Richard Roundtree
Jimmy Smits
John Tesh

In her first film, the title role in LOLITA (MGM, 1962), Sue Lyon held her own among a stellar cast. Bert Stern's photograph, with heart-shaped sunglasses and lollipop, brilliantly captures the tone of the entire film.

10

JOHN GILBERT
RON GLASS
FRED GWYNNE
SUE LYON

11

SALLY BLANE
YUL BRYNNER
TAB HUNTER
WALTER WANGER

12

KEITH ANDES
MILTON BERLE
BILL COSBY

13

BOB CRANE
HARRISON FORD
ROBERT FORSTER
RICHARD "CHEECH" MARIN

14

POLLY BERGEN
INGMAR BERGMAN
ROOSEVELT GRIER
NANCY OLSON
HARRY DEAN STANTON
TERRY-THOMAS
TOBY WING

Although Barbara Stanwyck appeared in a few really fine films, her many lesser vehicles are often regarded as classics because this consummate star made them sparkle. Here, with Dennis Morgan in CHRISTMAS IN CONNECTICUT *(Warner Bros., 1945).*

July

15

PHIL CAREY
ALEX KARRAS
JAN-MICHAEL VINCENT
PATRICK WAYNE

16

RUBEN BLADES
PHOEBE CATES
COREY FELDMAN
BERNARD HUGHES
PERCY KILBRIDE
GINGER ROGERS
BARBARA STANWYCK

17

LUCIE ARNAZ
JAMES CAGNEY
DIAHANN CARROLL
PHYLLIS DILLER
DAVID HASSELHOFF
ART LINKLETTER
DONALD SUTHERLAND

18

JAMES BROLIN
HUME CRONYN
AUDREY LANDERS
ELIZABETH MCGOVERN
HARRIET NELSON
RED SKELTON
LUPE VELEZ

19

LILI DAMITA
ANTHONY EDWARDS
PAT HINGLE
RICHARD JORDAN
PATRICIA MEDINA

Few people can say they've actually seen Theda Bara on the screen, yet, decades after her short career ended, the name (an anagram of "Arab Death") retains a life of its own. She remains the original vamp in films like A FOOL THERE WAS (Fox, 1914).

July

20

LOLA ALBRIGHT
THEDA BARA
SALLY ANN HOWES
DIANA RIGG
NATALIE WOOD

21

EDWARD HERRMANN
ART HINDLE
DON KNOTTS
JOHN LOVITZ
C. AUBREY SMITH
ROBIN WILLIAMS

22 SAXON TRAINOR - 1963

ALBERT BROOKS
RAYMOND CHANDLER
WILLEM DAFOE
DANNY GLOVER
JASON ROBARDS, JR.
ALEX TREBEK

23

CORAL BROWNE
GLORIA DEHAVEN
WOODY HARRELSON
TERENCE STAMP
ARTHUR TREACHER
MICHAEL WILDING

24 CHAD GUNN

RUTH BUZZI
LYNDA CARTER
ROBERT HAYES
CHRIS SARANDON

A deft blending of inductive crime solving and sophisticated domestic comedy in THE THIN MAN *series made William Powell and Myrna Loy immortal among successive generations of film viewers. Here, in* EVELYN PRENTICE *(MGM, 1934).*

July

25

WALTER BRENNAN
ESTELLE GETTY
JACK GILFORD
IMAN
LILA LEE
JANET MARGOLIN

26

GRACIE ALLEN
BLAKE EDWARDS
SUSAN GEORGE
MICK JAGGER
STANLEY KUBRICK
KEVIN SPACEY
VIVIAN VANCE

27

DONALD CRISP
BOBBIE GENTRY
NORMAN LEAR
NATALIE MOORHEAD
JOHN PLESHETTE
JERRY VAN DYKE
KEENAN WYNN

28

JOE E. BROWN
DARRYL HICKMAN
LINDA KELSEY
SALLY STRUTHERS
RUDY VALLEE

29

LLOYD BOCHNER
RICHARD EGAN
MARIA OUSPENSKAYA
WILLIAM POWELL
THELMA TODD
DAVID WARNER
WIL WHEATON

Mexico's most exotic export, Dolores Del Rio, was cast as a Russian beauty in this story set in America during the Civil War. THE MAN FROM DAKOTA (MGM, 1940) is also a viable action film with a bit of spying thrown in for good measure.

August

WILLIAM ATHERTON
PETER BOGDANOVICH
DELTA BURKE
KEN OLIN
ARNOLD SCHWARZENEGGER

30

MICHAEL BIEHN
GERALDINE CHAPLIN
GEORGE LIBERACE
DON MURRAY
FRANCE NUYEN

31   RANDY RENE '66

TEMPESTT BLEDSOE
DOM DeLUISE
GIANCARLO GIANNINI
ARTHUR HILL
LAURA JOHNSON
TAYLOR NEGRON

1

JOANNA CASSIDY
WES CRAVEN
KATHRYN HARROLD
MYRNA LOY
CARROLL O'CONNOR
PETER O'TOOLE
BEATRICE STRAIGHT

2

ALEX CORD
DOLORES DEL RIO
JEAN HAGEN
MARILYN MAXWELL
JAY NORTH
MARTIN SHEEN

3

Known for his minimalist acting style, Robert Mitchum has remained one of the busiest of actors for over fifty years. At left, typically the man of action, in Out of the Past *(RKO, 1947).*

August

4

David Brian
Helen Kane
Anita Page
Kristoffer Tabori

5

Loni Anderson
Anita Colby
Selma Diamond
John Huston
John Saxon
Robert Taylor

6

Lucille Ball
Paul Bartel
Hoot Gibson
Stepfanie Kramer
Robert Mitchum
Louella Parsons
Andy Warhol

7

Billie Burke
Anjanette Comer
Marlyn Mason

8

Rory Calhoun
Keith Carradine
Dustin Hoffman
Sylvia Sidney
Connie Stevens
Carl "Alfalfa" Switzer
Esther Williams

Norma Shearer's patrician demeanor fused with intense inner strength in her best roles to create a unique leading lady in the thirties. At left, the queen of MGM as queen of France in MARIE ANTOINETTE *(MGM, 1938).*

August

9
ROBERT ALDRICH
SAM ELLIOTT
CHARLES FARRELL
MELANIE GRIFFITH
WHITNEY HOUSTON
DOROTHY JORDAN
ROBERT SHAW

10
ROSANNA ARQUETTE
EDDIE FISHER
RHONDA FLEMING
JACK HALEY
MARTHA HYER
NORMA SHEARER

11
ARLENE DAHL
MIKE DOUGLAS
ANNA MASSEY
LLOYD NOLAN

12
CECIL B. DE MILLE
JOHN DEREK
GEORGE HAMILTON
SAM J. JONES
DEBORAH WALLEY
JANE WYATT

13
NEVILLE BRAND
PAT HARRINGTON
ALFRED HITCHCOCK
BERT LAHR
GENE RAYMOND
CHARLES "BUDDY" ROGERS

Mae West literally constituted a one-woman genre, whose brassy, self-assured, flawless comic timing was displayed in carefully tailored roles such as Mavis Arden in GO WEST YOUNG MAN *(Paramount, 1936).*

August

14 MARC ALAN RAPPAPORT. 1968

ANTONIO FARGAS
ALICE GHOSTLEY
JACKÉE
STEVE MARTIN
SUSAN SAINT JAMES
LENA WERTMULLER

15

ETHEL BARRYMORE
JULIA CHILD
MIKE CONNORS
LINDA ELLERBEE
DAME WENDY HILLER
ROSE MARIE
JANICE RULE

16

ANN BLYTHE
MAE CLARKE
ROBERT CULP
TIMOTHY HUTTON
MADONNA
JULIE NEWMAR
LESLEY ANN WARREN

17

ROBERT DE NIRO
MAUREEN O'HARA
SEAN PENN
ROMAN POLANSKI
MAE WEST
MONTE WOOLLEY

18

TRAVIS BANTON
MAX FACTOR
ROBERT REDFORD
CHRISTIAN SLATER
PATRICK SWAYZE
GRANT WILLIAMS
SHELLEY WINTERS

Often cited by critics and fans alike as the best musical ever filmed, SINGIN' IN THE RAIN (MGM, 1952) demonstrates the new vitality that star/choreographer Gene Kelly contributed to movie musicals of the golden age.

19

CLAUDE DAUPHIN
PETER GALLAGHER
GERALD McRANEY
DIANA MULDAUR
JILL ST. JOHN
JOHN STAMOS
MARIE WILSON

20

CONNIE CHUNG
PETER HORTON
JACQUELINE SUSANN

21

KIM CATTRALL
PATTY McCORMACK
KENNY ROGERS
MELVIN VAN PEEBLES
PETER WEIR
CLARENCE WILLIAMS III

22

ELISABETH BERGNER
VALERIE HARPER
DOROTHY PARKER
CINDY WILLIAMS

23

TONY BILL
BARBARA EDEN
GENE KELLY
SHELLEY LONG
VERA MILES
RIVER PHOENIX

Planned as a vehicle for Garbo, the story of Napoleon's mistress Maria Walewska had been shelved indefinitely for lack of a viable leading man. Casting of the superb Charles Boyer gave "Miss G" her first true costar in CONQUEST *(MGM, 1937).*

August

24

STEVE GUTTENBERG
DURWOOD KIRBY
MARLEE MATLIN

25

CLARA BOW
SEAN CONNERY
MEL FERRER
MONTY HALL
RUBY KEELER
MICHAEL RENNIE
TOM SKERRITT

26 TIM REED

MACAULAY CULKIN
BRETT CULLEN
JIM DAVIS
CHRISTOPHER ISHERWOOD
MAXWELL SHANE

27

CHARLES FLEISHER
SAMUEL GOLDWYN
PEE-WEE HERMAN
MARTHA RAYE
DIANA SCARWID
TUESDAY WELD

28

CHARLES BOYER
BEN GAZZARA
JAMES WONG HOWE
NANCY KULP
DONALD O'CONNOR
EMMA SAMMS
DAVID SOUL

Ingrid Bergman's innate ability to play either the virgin or the vixen is clearly intimated in her most famous role. As Ilsa Laszlo in CASABLANCA *(Warner Bros., 1942), she is torn between her admiration for one man and passion for another.*

August

29
INGRID BERGMAN
REBECCA DeMORNAY
WILLIAM FRIEDKIN
RICHARD GERE
MICHAEL JACKSON
JASON PRIESTLY
ISABEL SANFORD

30
ELIZABETH ASHLEY
JOAN BLONDELL
SHIRLEY BOOTH
TIMOTHY BOTTOMS
FRED MACMURRAY
RAYMOND MASSEY

31
RICHARD BASEHART
JAMES COBURN
ARTHUR GODFREY
BUDDY HACKETT
FREDRIC MARCH
WILLIAM SAROYAN
DORY SCHARY

1
BETTY BLYTHE
YVONNE DeCARLO
VITTORIO GASSMAN
JACK HAWKINS
GEORGE MAHARIS
LILY TOMLIN

SEPTEMBER

2
MARK HARMON
LINDA PURL
KEANU REEVES

Raquel Welch put aside her usual glamorous image for what is considered her best acting performance, a tough-rolling, tough-talking professional skater in KANSAS CITY BOMBER *(MGM, 1972).*

September

3

EILEEN BRENNAN
KITTY CARLISLE HART
ANNE JACKSON
ALAN LADD
VALERIE PERRINE
CHARLIE SHEEN

4

MITZI GAYNOR
GLORIA HOLDEN
JUDITH IVEY
HOWARD MORRIS
DICK YORK

5

WILLIAM DEVANE
CAROL LAWRENCE
BOB NEWHART
RAQUEL WELCH
DARRYL F. ZANUCK

6

JANE CURTIN
OTTO KRUGER
SWOOSIE KURTZ
BILLY ROSE

7

CORBIN BERNSEN
SUSAN BLAKELY
JULIE KAVNER
ELIA KAZAN
JOHN PHILLIP LAW
PETER LAWFORD
ANTHONY QUAYLE

Maurice Chevalier was enormously popular with American audiences when he played the "naughty-but-nice" foil opposite Jeanette MacDonald in Ernst Lubitsch's THE MERRY WIDOW *(MGM, 1934).*

September

8

JEAN-LOUIS BARRAULT
SID CAESAR
PATSY CLINE
DENISE DARCEL
VIRNA LISI
PETER SELLERS
HENRY WILCOXON

9

ANGELA CARTWRIGHT
JANE GREER
MICHAEL KEATON
JOSEPH E. LEVINE
SYLVIA MILES
CLIFF ROBERTSON
TOPOL

10

JUDY GEESON
AMY IRVING
GREG MULLAVEY
EDMOND O'BRIEN
YUMA SUMAC

11

BRIAN DE PALMA
LOLA FALANA
EARL HOLLIMAN
KRISTY MCNICHOL

12

MAURICE CHEVALIER
LINDA GRAY
IAN HOLM
PETER SCOLARI

In less than a year Lauren Bacall made it from the cover of Harper's Bazaar *to Hollywood and her first film (with Humphrey Bogart),* TO HAVE AND HAVE NOT *(Warner Bros., 1945). James Agee wrote that Bacall "had cinema personality to burn."*

September

BARBARA BAIN
JACQUELINE BISSET
SCOTT BRADY
NELL CARTER
CLAUDETTE COLBERT
MAURICE JARRE
MEL TORME

13

FAITH FORD
JOEY HEATHERTON
KAY MEDFORD
CLAYTON MOORE
JOE PENNY
HARVE PRESNELL
NICOL WILLIAMSON

14

JACKIE COOPER
WERNER HERZOG
TOMMY LEE JONES
MARGARET LOCKWOOD
PENNY SINGLETON
OLIVER STONE
FAY WRAY

15

LAUREN BACALL
ED BEGLEY, JR.
PETER FALK
ANNE FRANCIS
SIR ALEXANDER KORDA
JANIS PAIGE

16

ANNE BANCROFT
DOROTHY LOUDON
RODDY MCDOWALL
JOHN RITTER

17   LUPE MARMOLEJO 1958

Hollywood's supreme enigma, Greta Garbo, is shown here (sans Hollywood gilt) in a Ruth Harriet Louise photograph for A WOMAN OF AFFAIRS *(MGM, 1928). With this film Garbo modernized her acting style and continued to grow in popularity.*

September

E. "ROCHESTER" ANDERSON 18
FRANKIE AVALON
ROBERT BLAKE
ROSSANO BRAZZI
GRETA GARBO
MAY MCAVOY
JACK WARDEN

RICARDO CORTEZ 19 *CARRIE Abelson*
RAY DANTON
FRANCES FARMER
JEREMY IRONS
DAVID MCCALLUM
TWIGGY
ADAM WEST

DR. JOYCE BROTHERS 20
SOPHIA LOREN
ANNE MEARA
FERNANDO REY
RACHEL ROBERTS

DAWN ADDAMS 21
FANNIE FLAGG
HENRY GIBSON
LARRY HAGMAN
STEPHEN KING
RICKI LAKE
BILL MURRAY

SCOTT BAIO 22
SHARI BELAFONTE-HARPER
JOHN HOUSEMAN
PAUL MUNI
CATHERINE OXENBERG
ERICH VON STROHEIM

Mickey Rooney became an MGM contract player in 1934; by the early 1940s he had become the studio's top star. His engaging versatility shone in the ANDY HARDY *series and musical vehicles like* BABES ON BROADWAY *(MGM, 1941).*

September

23
RAY CHARLES
STANLEY KRAMER
PAUL PETERSEN
WALTER PIDGEON
MARY KAY PLACE
MICKEY ROONEY
ROMY SCHNEIDER

24
F. SCOTT FITZGERALD
JIM HENSON
ANTHONY NEWLEY
JEAN-CLAUDE PASCAL

25
MICHAEL DOUGLAS
MARK HAMILL
HEATHER LOCKLEAR
JULIET PROWSE
ALDO RAY
CHRISTOPHER REEVE
BARBARA WALTERS

26
MELISSA SUE ANDERSON
LINDA HAMILTON
MARY BETH HURT
JULIE LONDON
OLIVIA NEWTON-JOHN
PATRICK O'NEAL
GEORGE RAFT

27
SHAUN CASSIDY
WILLIAM CONRAD
A. MARTINEZ
JAYNE MEADOWS
SADA THOMPSON

Groucho Marx preens his perfect foil Margaret Dumont in A Night at the Opera *(MGM, 1935). Appearing together in seven films, his business with the monumental Dumont is often superior to that with Harpo and Chico.*

September

Brigitte Bardot
Peter Finch
Sylvia Kristel
Marcello Mastroianni
John Sales
Ed Sullivan
William Windom

28

Gene Autry
Anita Ekberg
Greer Garson
Trevor Howard
Madeline Kahn
Emily Lloyd
Lizabeth Scott

29

Truman Capote
Angie Dickenson
Deborah Kerr
Victoria Tennant

30

Julie Andrews
Laurence Harvey
Walter Matthau
George Peppard
Randy Quaid
Everett Sloane
Stella Stevens

1

OCTOBER

Bud Abbot
Moses Gunn
Groucho Marx
Rex Reed
Sting

2

Sophisticated wit shaded by personal charm and warmth, and high comedic finesse imbued with a subtle childlike glee, made Carole Lombard the queen of screwball comedy. Her beauty is evidenced here in THE GAY BRIDE *(MGM, 1934).*

3

GERTRUDE BERG
HART BOCHNER
WARNER OLAND
MADLYN RHUE
GORE VIDAL

4

ARMAND ASSANTE
FELICIA FARR
CHARLTON HESTON
BUSTER KEATON
JAN MURRAY
SUSAN SARANDON

5

KAREN ALLEN
BILL DANA
GLYNIS JOHNS
ALAN LUDDEN
DONALD PLEASANCE

6

SHANA ALEXANDER
BRITT EKLAND
JANET GAYNOR
CAROLE LOMBARD
STEPHANIE ZIMBALIST

7

JUNE ALLYSON
ANDY DIVINE
JUDY LANDERS
DIANA LYNN

*During her short stay in Hollywood, Helen Hayes
won an Oscar for her first film, and later starred
with Clark Gable in the "spirit versus flesh"
melodrama* THE WHITE SISTER *(MGM, 1933).*

October

RONA BARRETT
CHEVY CHASE
ROUBEN MAMOULIAN
DAMON RUNYON
SIGOURNEY WEAVER

8 CIRCE & GRAHAM

EDWARD ANDREWS
GARY FRANK
MICHAEL PARÉ
ALASTAIR SIM

9

HELEN HAYES
DANIEL MASSEY
ALAN RACHINS
BEN VEREEN

10

JOAN CUSACK
RON LEIBMAN
DAVID MORSE
LUKE PERRY

11

SUSAN ANTON
JOSEPHINE HUTCHINSON
STEFANIE POWERS
JEAN WALLACE

12

Rita Hayworth's striking beauty defined the look of the forties, as exemplified in the title role of GILDA *(Columbia, 1946). Her later films were rarely up to the quality of an ever-growing acting ability.*

October

13

LARAINE DAY
GLADYS GEORGE
JEAN HOWARD
YVES MONTAND
PAMELA TIFFIN
ROBERT WALKER
CORNEL WILDE

14

NOREEN CORCORAN
GREG EVIGAN
LILLIAN GISH
BENITA HUME
ROGER MOORE
ROBERT WEBBER

15

INA CLAIRE
MELVILLE COOPER
JANE DARWELL
LINDA LAVIN
MERVYN LEROY
PENNY MARSHALL
TANYA ROBERTS

16

REX BELL
LINDA DARNELL
ANGELA LANSBURY
TIM ROBBINS
SUZANNE SOMERS

17

JEAN ARTHUR
SPRING BYINGTON
MONTGOMERY CLIFT
BEVERLY GARLAND
RITA HAYWORTH
DOLPH LUNDGREN
IRENE RYAN

The epitome of cool, refined beauty, Catherine Deneuve is a member of the Doraléac acting family. Here she adds a touch of chic to an entertaining variation on the vampire legend in THE HUNGER *(MGM/UA, 1983).*

October

18

PETER BOYLE
PAM DAWBER
MIRIAM HOPKINS
MELINA MERCOURI
GEORGE C. SCOTT
INGER STEVENS
JEAN CLAUDE VAN DAMME

19

DIVINE
JOHN LITHGOW
TONY LO BIANCO
GEORGE NADER
ROBERT REED
SIMON WARD

20

EVELYN BRENT
MICHAEL DUNN
MARGARET DUMONT
ARLENE FRANCIS
BELA LUGOSI
DAME ANNA NEAGLE

21

CARRIE FISHER
JOYCE RANDOLPH
RUTH TERRY

22

CONSTANCE BENNETT
CATHERINE DENEUVE
JOAN FONTAINE
ANNETTE FUNICELLO
DEREK JACOBI
CHRISTOPHER LLOYD
BOOTS MALLORY

Anthony Franciosa's Broadway success led to a career as a popular leading man in movies and television. His first film role was in THIS COULD BE THE NIGHT (MGM, 1957).

October

23

ROBERT BRAY
JOHNNY CARSON
JORDAN CHRISTOPHER
DIANA DORS
UNA O'CONNOR

24

F. MURRAY ABRAHAM
PRESTON FOSTER
GILDA GRAY
MOSS HART
KEVIN KLINE
DAVID NELSON
DAME SYBIL THORNDIKE

25

BILLY BARTY
SARAH BERNHARDT
ANTHONY FRANCIOSA
ANNIE GIRARDOT
MINNIE PEARL

26

JACKIE COOGAN
CARY ELWES
PAT SAJAK
JACLYN SMITH

27

FANNY BRICE
JACK CARSON
JOHN CLEESE
RUBY DEE
NANETTE FABRAY
PETER FIRTH
CARRIE SNODGRESS

Ethel Waters is irresistible as Petunia Jackson,
fighting to save the soul of her "backslidin'"
husband Little Joe, in one of the most effective
musical fantasies ever filmed, CABIN IN THE SKY
(MGM, 1943).

October

28

JANE ALEXANDER
DODY GOODMAN
EDITH HEAD
ELSA LANCHESTER
SUZY PARKER
JOAN PLOWRIGHT
JULIA ROBERTS

29

GERALDINE BROOKS
RICHARD DREYFUSS
KATE JACKSON
WINONA RYDER

30

RUTH GORDON
HARRY HAMLIN
RUTH HUSSEY
CLAUDE LELOUCH
LOUIS MALLE
HENRY WINKLER

31

BARBARA BEL GEDDES
JOHN CANDY
DALE EVANS
LEE GRANT
SALLY KIRKLAND
DAVID OGDEN STIERS
ETHEL WATERS

---

1   NOVEMBER

ROBERT FOXWORTH
LAURA LA PLANTE
BETSY PALMER

Vivien Leigh twice won the Oscar and the New York Film Critics award for the same film, yet her mesmerizing presence often distracted viewers from truly appreciating the deftness of her acting. Here, in WATERLOO BRIDGE *(MGM, 1940).*

November

BURT LANCASTER
ANN RUTHERFORD
LUCHINO VISCONTI

2

ADAM ANT
ROSANNE ARNOLD
CHARLES BRONSON
STEVE LANDESBERG
LULU
MONICA VITTI

3

MARTIN BALSAM
ART CARNEY
DARLA HOOD
KATE REID
WILL ROGERS
LORETTA SWIT
GIG YOUNG

4

VIVIEN LEIGH
JOEL MCCREA
TATUM O'NEAL
ROY ROGERS
NATALIE SHAFER
SAM SHEPARD
ELKE SOMMER

5

BRAD DAVIS
SALLY FIELD
JUANITA HALL
FRANCIS LEDERER
MIKE NICHOLS
MARIA SHRIVER

6

Richard Burton's often quirky choice of film roles contributed to his reputation as "a great talent wasted"—at the expense of a few of the best performances on film. At left, in MY COUSIN RACHEL *(Twentieth Century-Fox, 1952).*

November

7
DEAN JAGGER
LEATRICE JOY
DANA PLATO

8
ALAIN DELON
MARY HART
JUNE HAVOC
PATTI PAGE
ESTHER ROLLE
ALFRE WOODARD

9
MARIE DRESSLER
LOU FERRIGNO
HEDY LAMARR
EDNA MAY OLIVER
ED WYNN

10
RICHARD BURTON
CLAUDE RAINS
JACK SCALIA
ROY SCHEIDER

11
BIBI ANDERSSON
KIM HUNTER
SUSAN KOHNER
DEMI MOORE
ROBERT RYAN
JONATHAN WINTERS
ROLAND YOUNG

One of Hitchcock's favorite "cool blondes," Grace Kelly was directed by the master in three of her eleven films. Her last picture, HIGH SOCIETY (MGM, 1956), was enormously popular during her royal romance.

November

12

INA BALIN
KIM HUNTER
GRACE KELLY

13

HERMIONE BADDELEY
LINDA CHRISTIAN
WHOOPI GOLDBERG
RICHARD MULLIGAN
JEAN SEBERG
MADELEINE SHERWOOD
OSKAR WERNER

14

LOUISE BROOKS
ROSEMARY DeCAMP
BRIAN KEITH
VERONICA LAKE
DICK POWELL

15

ED ASNER
PETULA CLARK
BEVERLY D'ANGELO
IRENE
JOHN KERR
LOUIS STONE
SAM WATERSTON

16

LISA BONET
ROYAL DANO
BURGESS MEREDITH
MABEL NORMAND
JOANNA PETTET
MARTHA PLIMPTON
GUY STOCKWELL

Beginning with good looks and no experience, Rock Hudson relied on tenacity and hard work to soon make him a top leading man. Moving from melodrama to adventure to comedy, he is shown here in SOMETHING OF VALUE *(MGM, 1957).*

November

17

DANNY DEVITO
ROCK HUDSON
LAUREN HUTTON
M. E. MASTRANTONIO
WILLIAM R. MOSES
MARTIN SCORSESE
LEE STRASBERG

18

IMOGENE COCA
LINDA EVANS
DAVID HEMMINGS
JAMESON PARKER
ELIZABETH PERKINS
BRENDA VACCARO

19

NANCY CARROLL
DICK CAVETT
JODIE FOSTER
GLYNNIS O'CONNOR
MEG RYAN
TED TURNER
CLIFTON WEBB

20

KAYE BALLARD
ALISTAIR COOKE
BO DEREK
VERONICA HAMMEL
ESTELLE PARSONS
GENE TIERNEY
SEAN YOUNG

21

GOLDIE HAWN
LORNA LUFT
HARPO MARX
RALPH MEEKER
HAROLD RAMIS
NICOLLETTE SHERIDAN
MARLO THOMAS

Bearing one of the most famous names in horror, Boris Karloff (with "made-to-order mate," Elsa Lanchester), is shown here in the truly off-beat genre classic THE BRIDE OF FRANKENSTEIN *(Universal, 1935).*

November

22
JAMIE LEE CURTIS
RODNEY DANGERFIELD
STEPHEN GEOFFREYS
TERRY GILLIAM
MARIEL HEMINGWAY
GERALDINE PAGE
RAY WALSTON

23
MAXWELL CAULFIELD
VICTOR JORY
BORIS KARLOFF
DAVID RAPPAPORT

24
HOWARD DUFF
GERALDINE FITZGERALD
GARSON KANIN
CATHLEEN NESBITT

25
CHRISTINA APPLEGATE
CURTIS BALDWIN
JEFFREY HUNTER
JESSE ROYCE LANDIS
JOHN LARROQUETTE
RICARDO MONTALBAN

26
FRANCES DEE
ROBERT GOULET
RICH LITTLE
TINA TURNER
EMLYN WILLIAMS

Gloria Grahame's distinctive voice, animal movement, and trademark pout combined to create star quality. Having won an Oscar for THE BAD AND THE BEAUTIFUL, *she is shown here in* COBWEB *(MGM, 1955).*

November

27

ROBIN GIVENS
ADELE JERGENS
BRUCE LEE
FISHER STEVENS
MONA WASHBOURNE
JALEEL WHITE

28

ALEXANDER GODUNOV
GLORIA GRAHAME
ED HARRIS
HOPE LANGE
JUDD NELSON
PAUL SHAFFER

29

BUSBY BERKELEY
DAGMAR
DIANE LADD
ROD LA ROCQUE
ANDREW McCARTHY
HOWIE MANDEL

30

DICK CLARK
RICHARD CRENNA
ROBERT GUILLAUME
VIRGINIA MAYO
ROBERT VAUGHN
EFREM ZIMBALIST, JR.

---

1   DECEMBER

WOODY ALLEN
MARY MARTIN
BETTE MIDLER
RICHARD PRYOR
DICK SHAWN
CHARLENE TILTON
TREAT WILLIAMS

Agnes Moorehead played various embodiments of the domineering woman in her radio, stage, film, and television career. At left, as the baleful spinster in THE MAGNIFICENT AMBERSONS *(RKO, 1942).*

December

2
STEVEN BAUER
DENNIS CHRISTOPHER
CATHY LEE CROSBY
ADOLPH GREEN
JULIE HARRIS
WARREN WILLIAM

3
MELODY ANDERSON
PAUL BERN
JEAN-LUC GODARD

4
MAX BAER, JR.
JEFF BRIDGES
HORST BUCHHOLTZ
DEANNA DURBIN
WINK MARTINDALE

5
WALT DISNEY
NUNNALLY JOHNSON
FRITZ LANG
GRACE MOORE
OTTO PREMINGER
GEORGE SAVALAS

6
WALLY COX
IRA GERSHWIN
TOM HULCE
LISSA LANDI
AGNES MOOREHEAD
JAMES NAUGHTON
JANINE TURNER

Margaret Hamilton in her most enduring role, as the "Wicked Witch of the West" in THE WIZARD OF OZ (MGM, 1939), pursued the fabled ruby slippers with a masterful vengeance.

December

7

GREG ALLMAN
FAY BAINTER
ELLEN BURSTYN
ROD CAMERON
C. THOMAS HOWELL
TED KNIGHT
ELI WALLACH

8

KIM BASINGER
DAVID CARRADINE
LEE J. COBB
SAMMY DAVIS, JR.
JOHN RUBINSTEIN
MAXIMILIAN SCHELL
FLIP WILSON

9

BEAU BRIDGES
KIRK DOUGLAS
DOUGLAS FAIRBANKS, JR.
REDD FOXX
HERMIONE GINGOLD
MARGARET HAMILTON
JOHN MALKOVICH

10

DAN BLOCKER
TIM CONSIDINE
SUSAN DEY
DOROTHY LAMOUR
UNA MERKEL
DENNIS MORGAN

11

TERI GARR
JEAN MARAIS
DONNA MILLS
RITA MORENO
CARLO PONTI
SUSAN SEIDLMAN
MARIE WINDSOR

At once genteel and sensual, Lee Remick
played a wide range of roles with conviction
and success. At left in her first film, A FACE
IN THE CROWD *(Warner Bros., 1957).*

December

12

ANA ALICIA
CONNIE FRANCIS
EDWARD G. ROBINSON
FRANK SINATRA
DIONNE WARWICK

13

VAN HEFLIN
DREW PEARSON
CHRISTOPHER PLUMMER
LILLIAN ROTH
DICK VAN DYKE

14

MOREY AMSTERDAM
DAN DAILEY
PATTY DUKE
LEE REMICK
DEE WALLACE STONE

15

MAXWELL ANDERSON
JEFF CHANDLER
TIM CONWAY
DON JOHNSON
HELEN SLATER

16

HARDIE ALBRIGHT
SIR NOËL COWARD
BEN CROSS
BARBARA KENT
TERENCE KNOX
LIV ULLMANN

There has never been anything predictable about Jane Fonda's career. For example, one of her best early performances was in a comedy by Tennessee Williams, who is noted for wrenching dramas. At left, in PERIOD OF ADJUSTMENT *(MGM, 1962).*

December

17
EUGENE LEVY
RICHARD LONG
RICHARD SALE
TOMMY STEELE

18
DAME GLADYS COOPER
OSSIE DAVIS
BETTY GRABLE
LEONARD MALTIN
ROGER SMITH
STEVEN SPIELBERG
GEORGE STEVENS

19
EDWARD PURDOM
TIM REID
SIR RALPH RICHARDSON
DAVID SUSSKIND
CECILY TYSON
ROBERT URICH

20
JENNY AGUTTER
CHARLIE CALLAS
IRENE DUNNE
AUDREY TOTTER

21
PHIL DONAHUE
JANE FONDA
BARRY GORDON
JARED MARTIN
JOSHUA MOSTEL
KIEFER SUTHERLAND

Ava Gardner's earthy sensuality and great beauty made her a reigning sex symbol, unsurpassed until the ascent of Marilyn Monroe. Early on she appeared in the Ann Sothern vehicle Maisie Goes to Reno *(MGM, 1944).*

December

22
Dame Peggy Ashcroft
Barbara Billinglsey
Hector Elizondo
Ruth Roman
Lynne Thigpen

23
Eric Blore
Richard Cromwell
Frederic Forrest
Harry Gardino
Elizabeth Hartman
Susan Lucci

24
Ruth Chatterton
Michael Curtiz
Ava Gardner
Howard Hughes

25
Rich Little
Tony Martin
Ismael Merchant
Joseph Schenck
Rod Serling
Sissy Spacek
Helen Twelvetrees

26
Steve Allen
Elisha Cook, Jr.
Alan King
Henry Miller
Richard Widmark

To Kismet (1944), MGM's escapist romp through old Bagdad, Marlene Dietrich added her stylized glamour and perpetual seduction. As Jamilla she painted her famous legs gold for her first filmed dance sequence.

December

27

Gérard Depardieu
Marlene Dietrich
Tovah Feldshuh
Sydney Greenstreet
Oscar Levant

28

Lew Ayres
Lee Bowman
Martin Milner
Hildegarde Neff
Dame Maggie Smith
Denzel Washington

29

Ted Danson
Ed Flanders
Viveca Lindfors
Mary Tyler Moore
Barbara Steele
Inga Swenson
Jon Voight

30

Jack Lord
Barbara Nichols
Bert Parks
Russ Tamblyn
Tracey Ullman
Jo Van Fleet
Fred Ward

31

Joe Dallesandro
Sir Anthony Hopkins
Val Kilmer
Ben Kingsley
Sarah Miles
Pola Negri
Orry-Kelly

INDEX OF BIRTHDAYS BY NAME

■ ■ ■

Abbot, Bud, 10/2/1895
Abbot, George, 6/25/1887
Abraham, F. Murray, 10/24/40
Ackland, Joss, 2/29/28
Ackroyd, Dan, 7/1/40
Adams, Brooke, 2/8/49
Adams, Don, 4/13/26
Adams, Edie, 4/16/23
Addams, Dawn, 9/21/30
Adjani, Isabelle, 6/27/55
Adrian, 3/3/03
Adrian, Iris, 5/29/13
Agutter, Jenny, 12/20/52
Aherne, Brian, 5/2/02
Aiello, Danny, 6/20/33
Aimée, Anouk, 4/27/32
Albert, Eddie, 4/22/08
Albert, Edward, 2/20/51
Albertson, Jack, 6/16/10
Albright, Hardie, 12/16/03
Albright, Lola, 7/20/25
Alda, Alan, 1/28/36
Aldrich, Robert, 8/9/18
Alexander, Jane, 10/28/39
Alexander, Shana, 10/6/25
Alicia, Ana, 12/12/56
Allen, Debbie, 1/16/50
Allen, Gracie, 7/26/02
Allen, Karen, 10/5/51
Allen, Nancy, 6/24/50
Allen, Steve, 12/26/21
Allen, Woody, 12/1/35
Alley, Kirstie, 1/12/55
Allman, Greg, 12/7/–
Allyson, June, 10/7/17
Altman, Robert, 2/20/25
Ameche, Don, 5/31/08
Amsterdam, Morey, 12/14/12
Anderson, Eddie "Rochester,"
    9/18/05
Anderson, Dame Judith,
    2/10/1898
Anderson, Kevin, 1/13/60
Anderson, Loni, 8/5/45
Anderson, Maxwell,
    12/15/1888
Anderson, Melissa Sue,
    9/26/62
Anderson, Melody, 12/3/55
Anderson, Warner, 3/10/11
Andersson, Bibi, 11/11/35
Andes, Keith, 7/12/20
Andress, Ursula, 3/19/36

Andrews, Dana, 1/1/09
Andrews, Edward, 10/9/14
Andrews, Julie, 10/1/35
Angeli, Pier, 6/19/32
Annis, Francesca, 5/14/44
Ann-Margret, 4/28/41
Ant, Adam, 11/3/–
Anton, Susan, 10/12/50
Applegate, Christina, 11/25/71
Arbuckle, R. "Fatty,"
    3/24/1887
Arden, Eve, 4/30/12
Arkin, Alan, 3/26/34
Arliss, George, 4/10/1868
Armstrong, Louis, 7/4/1900
Arnaz, Desi, Sr., 3/2/17
Arnaz, Desi, Jr., 1/19/53
Arnaz, Lucie, 7/17/51
Arness, James, 5/26/23
Arnold, Edward, 2/18/1890
Arnold, Rosanne, 11/3/52
Arquette, Rosanna, 8/10/59
Arthur, Beatrice, 5/13/24
Arthur, Jean, 10/17/05
Ashcroft, Dame Peggy,
    12/22/07
Ashley, Elizabeth, 8/30/39
Asner, Ed, 11/15/29
Assante, Armand, 10/4/49
Astaire, Fred, 5/10/1899
Astin, John, 3/30/30
Astor, Mary, 5/3/06
Atherton, William, 7/30/47
Atkins, Christopher, 2/21/61
Aumont, Jean-Pierre, 1/5/09
Autry, Gene, 9/29/07
Avalon, Frankie, 9/18/39
Axelrod, George, 6/9/22
Axton, Hoyt, 3/25/38
Ayres, Lew, 12/28/08

Bacall, Lauren, 9/16/24
Backus, Jim, 2/25/13
Bacon, Kevin, 7/8/58
Baddeley, Hermione, 11/13/06
Baer, Max, Jr., 12/4/37
Bailey, Pearl, 3/29/18
Bain, Barbara, 9/13/31
Bainter, Fay, 12/7/1892
Baio, Scott, 9/22/61
Baker, Carroll, 5/28/31
Baker, Diane, 2/25/38
Baker, Joe Don, 2/12/43

Baker, Josephine, 6/3/06
Baldwin, Alec, 4/3/58
Baldwin, Curtis, 11/25/67
Balin, Ina, 11/12/37
Ball, Lucille, 8/6/11
Ballard, Kaye, 11/20/26
Balsam, Martin, 11/4/19
Bancroft, Anne, 9/17/31
Bankhead, Tallulah, 1/31/03
Banky, Vilma, 1/9/1898
Bannen, Ian, 6/29/28
Banton, Travis, 8/18/1894
Bara, Theda, 7/20/1890
Barbeau, Adrienne, 6/11/47
Barbera, Joseph, 3/24/11
Bardot, Brigitte, 9/28/34
Barker, Lex, 5/8/19
Barkin, Ellen, 4/16/54
Barnes, Binnie, 3/25/05
Barrault, Jean-Louis, 9/8/10
Barrett, Rona, 10/8/36
Barrie, Barbara, 5/23/31
Barris, Chuck, 6/3/29
Barry, Gene, 6/14/21
Barrymore, Diana, 3/3/21
Barrymore, Drew, 2/22/75
Barrymore, Ethel, 8/15/1879
Barrymore, John, 2/15/1882
Barrymore, Lionel, 4/28/1878
Bartel, Paul, 8/6/38
Barthelmess, Richard,
    5/9/1895
Bartholomew, Freddie,
    3/28/24
Barty, Billy, 10/25/24
Baryshnikov, Mikhail, 1/27/48
Basehart, Richard, 8/31/14
Basinger, Kim, 12/8/53
Bateman, Jason, 1/14/69
Bateman, Justine, 2/19/66
Bates, Alan, 2/17/34
Bates, Kathy, 6/28/48
Bauer, Steven, 12/2/56
Baxter, Anne, 5/7/23
Baxter, Meredith, 6/21/47
Baxter, Warner, 3/29/1891
Beaton, Cecil, 1/14/04
Beatty, Clyde, 6/10/03
Beatty, Ned, 7/6/37
Beatty, Warren, 3/30/37
Beaumont, Hugh, 2/16/09
Beavers, Louise, 3/8/02
Beck, Michael, 2/4/49

Bedelia, Bonnie, 3/25/46
Beecham, Stephanie, 2/28/–
Beery, Wallace, 4/1/1885
Begley, Ed, Sr., 3/25/01
Begley, Ed, Jr., 9/16/49
Belafonte, Harry, 3/1/27
Belafonte-Harper, Shari,
    9/22/54
Bel Geddes, Barbara, 10/31/22
Bell, Rex, 10/16/05
Bellamy, Madge, 6/30/1900
Bellamy, Ralph, 6/17/04
Beller, Kathleen, 2/10/55
Bellwood, Pamela, 6/26/51
Belmondo, Jean-Paul, 4/9/33
Belushi, James, 6/15/54
Belushi, John, 1/24/49
Benaderet, Bea, 4/4/06
Bendix, William, 1/4/06
Bening, Annette, 5/29/58
Benjamin, Richard, 5/22/38
Bennett, Bruce, 5/19/09
Bennett, Constance, 10/22/04
Bennett, Joan, 2/27/10
Benny, Jack, 2/14/1894
Benson, Robby, 1/21/56
Benton, Barbi, 1/28/50
Berenger, Tom, 5/31/50
Berenson, Marisa, 2/15/48
Berg, Gertrude, 10/3/1899
Bergen, Candice, 5/9/46
Bergen, Edgar, 2/16/03
Bergen, Polly, 7/14/30
Berger, Helmut, 5/29/44
Berger, Senta, 5/13/41
Bergman, Ingmar, 7/14/18
Bergman, Ingrid, 8/29/13
Bergner, Elisabeth, 8/22/1900
Berkeley, Busby, 11/29/1895
Berle, Milton, 7/12/08
Berman, Shelley, 2/3/26
Bern, Paul, 12/3/1889
Bernhard, Sandra, 6/6/55
Bernhardt, Sarah, 10/25/1844
Bernsen, Corbin, 9/7/54
Bertinelli, Valerie, 4/23/60
Bertolucci, Bernardo, 3/16/40
Besch, Bibi, 2/1/42
Bessell, Ted, 3/20/35
Best, Edna, 3/3/1900
Betz, Carl, 3/9/20
Bey, Turhan, 3/30/20
Beymer, Richard, 2/21/39

Bickford, Charles, 1/1/1889
Biehn, Michael, 7/31/56
Bill, Tony, 8/23/40
Billingsley, Barbara, 12/22/22
Bishop, Joey, 2/3/19
Bisset, Jacqueline, 9/13/44
Black, Karen, 7/1/42
Blades, Ruben, 7/16/48
Blair, Janet, 4/23/21
Blair, Linda, 1/22/59
Blake, Amanda, 2/20/29
Blake, Robert, 9/18/33
Blakely, Susan, 9/7/50
Blane, Sally, 7/11/10
Blanc, Mel, 5/30/08
Bledsoe, Tempestt, 8/1/73
Blocker, Dan, 12/10/32
Blondell, Joan, 8/30/09
Bloom, Claire, 2/15/31
Blore, Eric, 12/23/1887
Blythe, Ann, 8/16/28
Blythe, Betty, 9/1/1893
Bochner, Hart, 10/3/56
Bochner, Lloyd, 7/29/24
Bogarde, Dirk, 3/28/20
Bogart, Humphrey, 1/23/1899
Bogdanovich, Peter, 7/30/39
Bolger, Ray, 1/10/04
Bond, Ward, 4/9/03
Bondi, Beulah, 5/3/1892
Bonet, Lisa, 11/16/67
Bono, Sonny, 2/16/35
Booth, Shirley, 8/30/07
Borga, Victor, 1/3/09
Borgnine, Ernest, 1/24/17
Bostwick, Barry, 2/24/45
Bottoms, Joseph, 4/22/54
Bottoms, Timothy, 8/30/50
Bow, Clara, 8/25/05
Bowie, David, 1/8/47
Bowman, Lee, 12/28/14
Boxleitner, Bruce, 5/12/50
Boyd, William, 6/5/1898
Boyer, Charles, 8/28/1897
Boyle, Peter, 10/18/33
Bracken, Eddie, 2/7/20
Brady, Scott, 9/13/24
Brand, Neville, 8/13/21
Brand, Oscar, 2/7/20
Brandauer, Klaus Maria,
 6/22/44
Brando, Marlon, 4/3/24
Bray, Robert, 10/23/17
Brazzi, Rossano, 9/18/16
Brennan, Eileen, 9/3/37
Brennan, Walter, 7/25/1894
Brent, Evelyn, 10/20/1899
Brent, George, 3/15/04
Brian, David, 8/4/14

Brian, Mary, 2/17/08
Brice, Fanny, 10/27/1891
Bridges, Beau, 12/9/41
Bridges, Jeff, 12/4/49
Bridges, Lloyd, 1/15/13
Brinkley, Christie, 2/2/54
Broderick, James, 3/6/30
Broderick, Matthew, 3/21/62
Brolin, James, 7/18/40
Bronson, Charles, 11/3/21
Brooks, Albert, 7/22/47
Brooks, Geraldine, 10/29/25
Brooks, Louise, 11/14/22
Brooks, Mel, 6/28/26
Brosnan, Pierce, 5/16/52
Brothers, Dr. Joyce, 9/20/28
Brown, Joe E., 7/28/1892
Brown, Roscoe Lee, 5/2/25
Browne, Coral, 7/23/13
Bryan, Dora, 2/7/24
Bryan, Jane, 6/11/18
Brynner, Yul, 7/11/15
Buchholtz, Horst, 12/4/32
Buckley, Betty, 7/3/47
Bujold, Geneviève, 7/1/42
Buñuel, Louis, 2/22/1900
Burke, Billie, 8/7/1885
Burke, Delta, 7/30/56
Burnett, Carol, 4/26/33
Burns, George, 1/20/1896
Burr, Raymond, 5/21/17
Burstyn, Ellen, 12/7/32
Burton, LeVar, 2/16/57
Burton, Richard, 11/10/25
Busey, Gary, 6/29/44
Bushman, Francis X.,
 1/10/1883
Buttons, Red, 2/5/19
Buzzi, Ruth, 7/24/36
Byington, Spring, 10/17/1893

Caan, James, 3/26/39
Cabot, Bruce, 4/20/04
Caesar, Sid, 9/8/22
Cage, Nicholas, 1/7/64
Cagney, James, 7/17/1899
Caine, Michael, 3/14/33
Calhoun, Rory, 8/8/22
Callas, Charlie, 12/20/–
Calvet, Corine, 4/30/25
Cambridge, Godfrey, 2/26/33
Cameron, Rod, 12/7/10
Campbell, Glen, 4/22/35
Candy, John, 10/31/50
Cannon, Dyan, 1/4/39
Cantor, Eddie, 1/31/1892
Capote, Truman, 9/30/24
Capra, Frank, 5/18/1897
Capucine, 1/6/33

Cara, Irene, 3/18/59
Cardinale, Claudia, 4/15/39
Carey, Macdonald, 3/15/13
Carey, Phil, 7/15/25
Carlin, George, 5/12/37
Carney, Art, 11/4/18
Caron, Leslie, 7/1/31
Carpenter, Karen, 3/2/50
Carradine, David, 12/8/36
Carradine, John, 2/5/06
Carradine, Keith, 8/8/51
Carradine, Robert, 3/24/45
Carroll, Diahann, 7/17/35
Carroll, Madeleine, 2/26/06
Carroll, Nancy, 11/19/04
Carson, Jack, 10/27/10
Carson, Johnny, 10/23/25
Carter, Dixie, 5/25/39
Carter, Jack, 6/24/23
Carter, Lynda, 7/24/51
Carter, Nell, 9/13/48
Cartwright, Angela, 9/9/52
Carvey, Dana, 6/6/55
Cass, Peggy, 5/21/24
Cassidy, David, 4/12/50
Cassidy, Jack, 3/5/27
Cassidy, Joanna, 8/2/44
Cassidy, Shaun, 9/27/58
Cates, Phoebe, 7/16/63
Cattrall, Kim, 8/21/56
Caufield, Joan, 6/1/22
Caulfield, Maxwell, 11/23/59
Cavett, Dick, 11/19/36
Cellini, Karen, 5/13/–
Chamberlain, Richard,
 3/31/35
Chandler, Jeff, 12/15/18
Chandler, Raymond,
 7/22/1888
Chaney, Lon, Sr., 4/1/1883
Chaney, Lon, Jr., 2/10/06
Channing, Carol, 1/31/21
Channing, Stockard, 2/13/44
Chaplin, Sir Charles,
 4/16/1889
Chaplin, Geraldine, 7/31/44
Chaplin, Lita Grey, 4/15/08
Chapman, Graham, 1/8/40
Charisse, Cyd, 3/8/21
Charles, Ray, 9/23/18
Charo, 1/15/51
Chase, Chevy, 10/8/43
Chase, Ilka, 4/8/03
Chatterton, Ruth, 12/24/1893
Chevalier, Maurice, 9/12/1888
Cher, 5/20/46
Child, Julia, 8/15/12
Chong, Tommy, 5/24/38
Christian, Linda, 11/13/23

Christie, Julie, 4/14/41
Christopher, Dennis, 12/2/55
Christopher, Jordan, 10/23/40
Claire, Ina, 10/15/1892
Clark, Dick, 11/30/29
Clark, Petula, 11/15/32
Clark, Susan, 3/8/40
Clarke, Candy, 6/20/47
Clarke, Mae, 8/16/07
Clayburgh, Jill, 4/30/44
Cleese, John, 10/27/39
Clift, Montgomery, 10/17/20
Cline, Patsy, 9/8/32
Clive, Colin, 1/20/1898
Clooney, Rosemary, 5/23/28
Close, Glenn, 3/19/47
Cobb, Lee J., 12/8/11
Coburn, James, 8/31/28
Coca, Imogene, 11/18/08
Cochran, Steve, 5/25/17
Coco, James, 3/21/29
Cocteau, Jean, 7/5/1889
Cohan, George M., 7/3/1878
 (celebrated on 7/4)
Colbert, Claudette, 9/13/05
Colby, Anita, 8/15/14
Cole, Nat "King," 3/17/19
Coleman, Dabney, 1/2/32
Collier, Constance, 1/22/1878
Collins, Joan, 5/23/33
Colman, Ronald, 2/9/1891
Comden, Betty, 5/3/19
Comer, Anjanette, 8/7/42
Como, Perry, 5/18/12
Compton, Joyce, 1/27/07
Connery, Sean, 8/25/30
Connors, Chuck, 3/10/21
Connors, Mike, 8/15/25
Conrad, Robert, 3/1/35
Conrad, William, 9/27/20
Conried, Hans, 4/15/17
Considine, Tim, 12/10/41
Conte, Richard, 3/24/14
Converse, Frank, 5/22/38
Conway, Tim, 12/15/33
Coogan, Jackie, 10/26/14
Cook, Elisha, Jr., 12/26/04
Cooke, Alistair, 11/20/08
Cooper, Gary, 5/7/01
Cooper, Dame Gladys,
 12/18/1888
Cooper, Jackie, 9/15/21
Cooper, Melville, 10/15/1896
Coote, Robert, 2/4/09
Coppola, Francis Ford, 4/7/39
Corcoran, Noreen, 10/14/43
Cord, Alex, 8/3/31
Corey, Wendell, 3/20/14
Corman, Roger, 4/5/26

Cort, Bud, 3/29/50
Cortesa, Valentina, 1/1/24
Cortez, Ricardo, 9/19/1899
Cosby, Bill, 7/12/37
Costello, Lou, 3/6/06
Costner, Kevin, 1/18/54
Cotten, Joseph, 5/15/05
Courtney, Tom, 2/25/37
Coward, Sir Noël,
 12/16/1899
Cox, Wally, 12/6/24
Crabbe, Buster, 2/17/07
Craig, James, 2/4/12
Crain, Jean, 5/25/25
Crane, Bob, 7/13/28
Craven, Wes, 8/2/39
Crawford, Joan, 3/23/04
Crenna, Richard, 11/30/26
Crisp, Donald, 7/27/1880
Cristal, Linda, 2/24/35
Cromwell, Richard,
 12/23/1888
Cronenberg, David, 3/15/43
Cronyn, Hume, 7/18/11
Crosby, Bing, 5/2/04
Crosby, Cathy Lee, 12/2/48
Cross, Ben, 12/16/48
Cruise, Tom, 7/3/62
Cruz, Brandon, 5/28/62
Cryer, Jon, 4/16/65
Crystal, Billy, 3/14/47
Cugat, Xavier, 1/1/1900
Cukor, George, 7/7/1899
Culkin, Macaulay, 8/26/80
Cullen, Brett, 8/26/–
Culp, Robert, 8/16/30
Cummings, Constance,
 5/15/10
Cummings, Robert, 6/9/08
Curry, Tim, 4/19/46
Curtin, Jane, 9/6/47
Curtis, Jamie Lee, 11/22/58
Curtis, Tony, 6/3/25
Curtiz, Michael, 12/24/1888
Cusack, Joan, 10/11/62
Cusack, John, 6/28/66
Cushing, Peter, 5/26/13

Dafoe, Willem, 7/22/55
Dagmar, 11/29/26
Dahl, Arlene, 8/11/24
Dailey, Dan, 12/14/14
Dali, Salvador, 3/11/04
Dallesandro, Joe, 12/31/48
Dalton, Timothy, 3/21/44
Daltrey, Roger, 3/1/45
Daly, Tyne, 2/21/47
Damita, Lili, 7/19/01
Damone, Vic, 6/12/28

Dana, Bill, 10/5/24
D'Angelo, Beverly, 11/15/53
Dangerfield, Rodney, 11/22/21
Daniels, Bebe, 1/14/01
Danner, Blythe, 2/3/43
Dano, Royal, 11/16/22
Danson, Ted, 12/29/47
Danton, Ray, 9/19/31
Danza, Tony, 4/21/51
Darby, Kim, 7/8/48
Darcel, Denise, 9/8/25
Darin, Bobby, 5/14/36
Darnell, Linda, 10/16/21
Darren, James, 6/8/36
Darrieux, Danielle, 5/1/17
Darwell, Jane, 10/15/1879
Da Silva, Howard, 5/4/09
Dauphin, Claude, 8/19/03
Davies, Marion, 1/3/1897
Davis, Ann B., 5/5/26
Davis, Bette, 4/5/08
Davis, Brad, 11/6/49
Davis, Geena, 1/21/57
Davis, Jim, 8/26/15
Davis, Joan, 6/29/07
Davis, Ossie, 12/18/17
Davis, Sami, 6/21/–
Davis, Sammy, Jr., 12/8/25
Dawber, Pam, 10/18/51
Day, Doris, 4/3/24
Day, Laraine, 10/13/17
Day Lewis, Daniel, 4/29/58
Dean, James, 2/8/31
DeCamp, Rosemary, 11/14/14
DeCarlo, Yvonne, 9/1/21
Dee, Frances, 11/26/07
Dee, Ruby, 10/27/24
Dee, Sandra, 4/23/42
DeHaven, Gloria, 7/23/24
De Havilland, Olivia, 7/1/16
Dell, Myrna, 3/5/24
Delon, Alain, 11/8/35
Del Rio, Dolores, 8/3/05
DeLuise, Dom, 8/1/33
Demarest, William, 2/27/1892
De Mille, Cecil B., 8/12/1881
DeMornay, Rebecca, 8/29/62
Deneuve, Catherine, 12/22/43
De Niro, Robert, 8/17/43
Dennehy, Brian, 7/9/40
Dennis, Sandy, 4/27/37
De Palma, Brian, 9/11/41
Depardieu, Gérard, 12/27/48
Depp, Johnny, 6/9/63
Derek, John, 8/12/26
Derek, Bo, 11/20/56
Dern, Bruce, 6/4/36
Dern, Laura, 2/10/67
De Sica, Vittorio, 7/7/02

Devane, William, 9/5/39
DeVito, Danny, 11/17/44
Dewhurst, Colleen, 6/3/26
De Wilde, Brandon, 4/9/42
DeWitt, Joyce, 4/23/49
Dey, Susan, 12/10/52
DeYoung, Cliff, 2/12/45
Diamond, Selma, 8/5/20
Dickenson, Angie, 9/30/31
Dietrich, Marlene, 12/27/01
Diller, Phyllis, 7/17/17
Dillman, Bradford, 4/14/30
Dillon, Matt, 2/18/64
Disney, Walt, 12/5/01
Divine, 10/19/45
 (a.k.a. Glenn Harris
 Milstead)
Divine, Andy, 10/7/–
Dobson, Kevin, 3/18/43
Doherty, Shannen, 4/12/71
Domergue, Faith, 6/16/25
Donahue, Elinor, 4/19/37
Donahue, Phil, 12/21/35
Donahue, Troy, 1/27/37
Donat, Robert, 3/18/05
Donnelly, Ruth, 5/17/1896
Dors, Diana, 10/23/31
D'Orsay, Fifi, 4/16/04
Douglas, Kirk, 12/9/16
Douglas, Melvyn, 4/5/01
Douglas, Michael, 9/25/44
Douglas, Mike, 8/11/25
Douglas, Paul, 4/11/07
Dourif, Brad, 3/18/50
Dow, Tony, 4/13/45
Down, Lesley-Anne, 3/17/54
Downey, Robert, Jr., 4/4/65
Dressler, Marie, 11/9/1869
Dreyfuss, Richard, 10/29/48
Dryer, Fred, 7/6/46
Duff, Howard, 11/24/17
Duffy, Julia, 6/27/50
Duffy, Patrick, 3/17/49
Duke, Patty, 12/14/46
Dullea, Keir, 5/30/36
Dumont, Margaret,
 10/20/1889
Dunaway, Faye, 1/14/41
Dunn, Michael, 10/20/34
Dunne, Griffin, 6/8/55
Dunne, Irene, 12/20/1898
Dunnock, Mildred, 1/25/06
Durante, Jimmy, 2/10/1893
Durbin, Deanna, 12/4/21
Durning, Charles, 2/28/33
Duryea, Dan, 1/23/07
Duvall, Robert, 1/5/31
Duvall, Shelley, 7/7/50
Dysart, Richard, 3/30/29

Eagles, Jeanne, 6/26/1894
Eastwood, Clint, 5/31/30
Ebsen, Buddy, 4/2/08
Eddy, Nelson, 6/29/01
Eden, Barbara, 8/23/34
Edwards, Anthony, 7/19/63
Edwards, Blake, 7/26/22
Edwards, Ralph, 6/13/13
Edwards, Vince, 7/9/28
Egan, Richard, 7/29/21
Eggar, Samantha, 3/5/39
Eichhorn, Lisa, 2/4/52
Eisenstein, Sergei, 1/23/1898
Ekberg, Anita, 9/29/31
Ekland, Britt, 10/6/42
Elg, Taina, 3/9/30
Elizondo, Hector, 12/22/36
Ellerbee, Linda, 8/15/44
Elliott, Sam, 8/9/44
Elwes, Cary, 10/26/62
Englund, Robert, 6/6/49
Estevez, Emilio, 5/12/62
Estrada, Erik, 3/16/49
Evans, Dale, 10/31/12
Evans, Dame Edith, 2/8/1888
Evans, Linda, 11/18/42
Evans, Maurice, 6/3/01
Everett, Chad, 6/11/36
Evigan, Greg, 10/14/53
Ewell, Tom, 4/29/09

Fabares, Shelley, 1/19/44
Fabian, 2/6/40
Fabray, Nanette, 10/27/20
Factor, Max, 8/18/04
Fairbanks, Douglas, Sr.,
 5/23/1883
Fairbanks, Douglas, Jr.,
 12/9/09
Fairchild, Morgan, 2/3/50
Falana, Lola, 9/11/43
Falk, Peter, 9/16/27
Fargas, Antonio, 8/14/46
Farmer, Frances, 9/19/13
Farr, Felicia, 10/4/32
Farrell, Charles, 8/9/01
Farrow, Mia, 2/9/45
Fawcett, Farrah, 2/2/46
Faye, Alice, 5/5/12
Feldman, Charles K., 4/26/04
Feldman, Corey, 7/16/71
Feldman, Marty, 7/8/38
Feldon, Barbara, 3/12/39
Feldshuh, Tovah, 12/27/53
Fellini, Federico, 1/20/20
Ferrell, Conchata, 3/28/43
Ferrer, José, 1/8/12
Ferrer, Mel, 8/25/17

Ferrigno, Lou, 11/9/52
Field, Sally, 11/6/46
Fields, W. C., 1/29/1879
Finch, Peter, 9/28/16
Finney, Albert, 5/9/36
Firth, Peter, 10/27/53
Fisher, Carrie, 10/21/56
Fisher, Eddie, 8/10/28
Fitzgerald, Barry, 3/10/1888
Fitzgerald, F. Scott, 9/24/1896
Fitzgerald, Geraldine, 11/24/14
Flagg, Fannie, 9/21/44
Flaherty, Joe, 6/21/40
Flanders, Ed, 12/29/34
Fleisher, Charles, 8/27/50
Fleming, Victor, 2/23/1883
Fleming, Rhonda, 8/10/23
Flynn, Errol, 6/20/09
Foch, Nina, 4/20/24
Fonda, Brigette, 1/27/–
Fonda, Henry, 5/16/05
Fonda, Jane, 12/21/37
Fonda, Peter, 2/23/39
Fontaine, Joan, 10/22/17
Ford, Faith, 9/14/64
Ford, Glenn, 5/1/16
Ford, Harrison, 7/13/42
Ford, John, 2/1/1895
Ford, Tennessee Ernie,
  2/13/19
Forrest, Frederic, 12/23/36
Forster, Robert, 7/13/41
Forsythe, John, 1/29/18
Fosse, Bob, 6/23/27
Fosse, Brigitte, 3/11/46
Foster, Jodie, 11/19/62
Foster, Meg, 5/14/49
Foster, Preston, 10/24/02
Fox, Edward, 4/13/37
Fox, James, 5/19/39
Fox, Michael J., 6/9/61
Foxworth, Robert, 11/1/41
Foxx, Redd, 12/9/22
Franciosa, Anthony, 10/25/28
Francis, Anne, 9/16/30
Francis, Arlene, 10/20/12
Francis, Connie, 12/12/38
Francis, Kay, 1/13/03
Franciscus, James, 1/31/34
Frank, Gary, 10/9/50
Frankenheimer, John, 2/19/30
Franklin, Bonnie, 1/6/44
Franklin, Pamela, 2/4/50
Franz, Arthur, 2/29/20
Frawley, William, 2/26/1887
Freeman, Mona, 6/9/26
Freeman, Morgan, 6/1/37
Frewer, Matt, 1/4/57
Friedken, William, 8/29/39

Frost, David, 4/7/39
Funicello, Annette, 10/22/42

Gable, Clark, 2/1/01
Gabor, Eva, 2/11/24
Gabor, Zsa Zsa, 2/6/20
Gallagher, Peter, 8/19/55
Gam, Rita, 4/2/28
Garbo, Greta, 9/18/05
Garcia, Andy, 4/12/48
Gardenia, Vincent, 1/7/22
Gardiner, Reginald, 2/27/03
Gardner, Ava, 12/24/22
Garfield, John, 3/4/13
Garland, Beverly, 10/17/26
Garland, Judy, 6/10/22
Garner, James, 4/7/28
Garr, Teri, 12/11/49
Garrett, Betty, 5/23/19
Garson, Greer, 9/29/08
Gassman, Vittorio, 9/1/22
Gavin, John, 4/8/28
Gaynor, Janet, 10/6/06
Gaynor, Mitzi, 9/4/30
Gazzara, Ben, 8/28/30
Geary, Anthony, 5/29/47
Geeson, Judy, 9/10/48
Gentry, Bobbie, 7/27/44
Geoffreys, Stephen, 11/22/64
George, Gladys, 10/13/1900
George, Susan, 7/26/50
Gere, Richard, 8/29/49
Gershwin, George, 9/26/1898
Gershwin, Ira, 12/6/1896
Getty, Estelle, 7/25/24
Ghostley, Alice, 8/14/26
Giannini, Giancarlo, 8/1/42
Gibbons, Cedric, 3/23/1893
Gibbs, Marla, 6/14/41
Gibson, Henry, 9/21/35
Gibson, Hoot, 8/6/1892
Gibson, Mel, 1/3/51
Gielgud, Sir John, 4/14/04
Gilbert, John, 7/10/1895
Gilbert, Melissa, 5/8/64
Gilford, Jack, 7/25/07
Gilliam, Terry, 11/22/40
Gingold, Hermione, 12/9/1897
Girardot, Annie, 10/25/31
Gish, Dorothy, 3/11/1898
Gish, Lillian, 10/14/1896
Givens, Robin, 11/27/64
Glass, Ron, 7/10/45
Glazer, Paul Michael, 3/25/43
Gleason, Jackie, 2/26/16
Glenn, Scott, 1/26/42
Gless, Sharon, 5/31/43
Glover, Danny, 7/22/47
Gobel, George, 5/20/19

Godard, Jean-Luc, 12/3/30
Goddard, Paulette, 6/3/11
Godfrey, Arthur, 8/31/03
Godunov, Alexander, 11/28/49
Goldberg, Whoopi, 11/13/49
Goldwyn, Samuel, 8/27/1882
Goodman, Dody, 10/28/15
Goodman, John, 6/20/52
Gordon, Barry, 12/21/48
Gordon, Gale, 2/2/06
Gordon, Ruth, 10/30/1896
Gossett, Louis, Jr., 5/27/36
Goulet, Robert, 11/26/33
Grable, Betty, 12/18/16
Grahame, Gloria, 11/28/25
Granger, Farley, 7/1/25
Granger, Stewart, 5/6/13
Grant, Cary, 1/18/04
Grant, Lee, 10/31/27
Granville, Bonita, 2/2/23
Graves, Peter, 3/18/25
Gray, Dolores, 6/7/24
Gray, Gilda, 10/24/01
Gray, Linda, 9/12/40
Grayson, Kathryn, 2/9/22
Green, Aldolph, 12/2/18
Greene, Ellen, 2/22/50
Greene, Lorne, 2/12/15
Greene, Shecky, 4/8/25
Greenstreet, Sydney,
  12/27/1879
Greenwood, Charlotte,
  6/25/1893
Greenwood, Joan, 3/4/21
Greer, Jane, 9/9/24
Grey, Joel, 4/11/32
Grier, Roosevelt, 7/14/32
Griffin, Merv, 7/6/25
Griffith, Andy, 6/1/26
Griffith, D. W., 1/22/1875
Griffith, Melanie, 8/9/57
Grimes, Tammy, 1/30/34
Grodin, Charles, 4/21/35
Guardino, Harry, 12/23/25
Guest, Christopher, 2/5/48
Guillaume, Robert, 11/30/27
Guinness, Sir Alec, 4/2/14
Gunn, Moses, 10/2/29
Guy, Jasmine, 3/10/63
Guttenberg, Steve, 8/24/58
Gwynne, Fred, 7/10/26

Hackett, Buddy, 8/31/24
Hackett, Joan, 5/1/42
Hackman, Gene, 1/30/31
Hagen, Jean, 8/3/23
Hagerty, Julie, 6/15/55
Hagman, Larry, 9/21/39
Hale, Barbara, 4/18/21

Haley, Jack, 8/10/1899
Hall, Arsenio, 2/12/58
Hall, Jerry, 7/2/56
Hall, Jon, 2/23/13
Hall, Juanita, 11/6/01
Hall, Monty, 8/25/23
Hamill, Mark, 9/25/52
Hamilton, George, 8/12/39
Hamilton, Linda, 9/26/57
Hamilton, Margaret, 12/9/02
Hamlin, Harry, 10/30/51
Hammel, Veronica, 11/20/–
Hammett, Dashiell, 5/27/1894
Hanks, Tom, 7/9/56
Hardin, Ty, 1/1/30
Hardwick, Sir Cedric,
  2/19/1883
Hardy, Oliver, 1/18/1892
Harlow, Jean, 3/3/11
Harmon, Mark, 9/2/51
Harper, Valerie, 8/22/40
Harrelson, Woody, 7/23/62
Harrington, Pat, 8/13/29
Harris, Ed, 11/28/50
Harris, Julie, 12/2/25
Harris, Neil Patrick, 6/15/–
Harrison, Gregory, 5/31/50
Harrison, Rex, 3/5/08
Harrold, Kathryn, 8/2/50
Hart, Kitty Carlisle, 9/3/14
Hart, Mary, 11/8/50
Hart, Moss, 10/24/04
Hartley, Mariette, 6/21/40
Hartman, David, 5/19/35
Hartman, Elizabeth, 12/23/41
Hasselhoff, David, 7/17/52
Hathaway, Henry, 3/13/1898
Hauer, Rutger, 1/23/44
Harvey, Laurence, 10/1/28
Havoc, June, 11/8/16
Hawkins, Jack, 9/1/10
Hawn, Goldie, 11/21/45
Hayes, George "Gabby,"
  5/7/1885
Hayes, Helen, 10/10/1900
Hayes, Peter Lind, 6/25/15
Hayes, Robert, 7/24/47
Hayward, Louis, 3/19/09
Hayward, Susan, 6/30/18
Hayworth, Rita, 10/17/18
Head, Edith, 10/28/07
Headly, Glenne, 3/13/55
Heard, John, 3/7/46
Hearst, Patty, 2/20/54
Heatherton, Joey, 9/14/44
Hecht, Ben, 2/28/1893
Heckart, Eileen, 3/29/19
Heflin, Van, 12/13/10
Helm, Bridgitte, 3/17/06

Helmond, Katherine, 7/5/34
Hemingway, Mariel, 11/22/61
Hemmings, David, 11/18/41
Hemsley, Sherman, 2/1/38
Henderson, Florence, 2/14/34
Henie, Sonja, 4/8/12
Henner, Marilu, 4/6/52
Henried, Paul, 1/10/08
Henson, Jim, 9/24/36
Hepburn, Audrey, 5/4/29
Hepburn, Katharine, 5/12/07
Herman, Pee Wee, 8/27/53
  (a.k.a. Paul Rubens)
Herrmann, Edward, 7/21/43
Hershey, Barbara, 2/5/48
Herzog, Werner, 9/15/42
Heston, Charlton, 10/4/23
Hewett, Christopher, 4/5/–
Hickman, Darryl, 7/28/31
Hickman, Dwayne, 5/18/34
Hill, Arthur, 8/1/22
Hill, Benny, 1/21/25
Hill, Steven, 2/24/22
Hill, Terence, 3/29/41
Hiller, Dame Wendy, 8/15/12
Hindle, Art, 7/21/48
Hines, Gregory, 2/14/46
Hingle, Pat, 7/19/23
Hirsch, Judd, 3/15/35
Hitchcock, Alfred, 8/13/1899
Hobel, Mara, 6/18/71
Hoffman, Dustin, 8/8/37
Holbrook, Hal, 2/17/25
Holden, Gloria, 9/4/08
Holden, William, 4/17/18
Holliday, Judy, 6/21/22
Holliday, Polly, 7/2/37
Holliman, Earl, 9/11/28
Holm, Celeste, 4/29/19
Holm, Ian, 9/12/31
Hood, Darla, 11/4/31
Hope, Bob, 5/29/03
Hopkins, Sir Anthony, 12/31/37
Hopkins, Miriam, 10/18/02
Hopper, Dennis, 5/17/36
Hopper, Hedda, 6/2/1890
Hopper, William, 1/26/15
Horne, Lena, 6/30/17
Horsley, Lee, 5/15/55
Horton, Edward Everett,
  3/18/1886
Horton, Peter, 8/20/–
Houghton, Katherine, 3/10/45
Houseman, John, 9/22/02
Houston, Whitney, 8/9/63
Howard, Jean, 10/13/10
Howard, Ken, 3/28/44
Howard, Leslie, 4/24/1893
Howard, Ron, 3/1/54

Howard, Trevor, 9/29/16
Howe, James Wong, 8/28/1899
Howell, C. Thomas, 12/7/67
Howes, Sally Ann, 7/20/30
Hubley, Season, 5/14/51
Hudson, Rochelle, 3/6/14
Hudson, Rock, 11/17/25
Hughes, Bernard, 7/16/15
Hughes, Howard, 12/24/05
Hulce, Tom, 12/6/53
Hume, Benita, 10/14/06
Hunt, Linda, 4/2/45
Hunter, Holly, 3/20/58
Hunter, Ian, 6/13/1900
Hunter, Jeffrey, 11/25/25
Hunter, Kim, 11/12/22
Hunter, Tab, 7/11/31
Huppert, Isabelle, 3/16/55
Hurrell, George, 6/1/04
Hurt, John, 1/22/40
Hurt, Mary Beth, 9/26/48
Hurt, William, 3/20/50
Hussey, Ruth, 10/30/14
Huston, Anjelica, 7/8/51
Huston, John, 8/5/06
Huston, Walter, 4/6/1884
Hutchins, Will, 5/5/32
Hutchinson, Josephine,
  10/12/04
Hutton, Betty, 2/26/21
Hutton, Jim, 5/31/33
Hutton, Lauren, 11/17/43
Hutton, Timothy, 8/16/60
Hyde-White, Wilfred, 5/12/03
Hyer, Martha, 8/10/24

Idle, Eric, 3/23/43
Iman, 7/25/55
Ince, Ralph, 1/16/1887
Ireland, Jill, 4/24/36
Ireland, John, 1/30/14
Irene, 11/15/01
Irons, Jeremy, 9/19/48
Irving, Amy, 9/10/53
Isherwood, Christopher,
  8/26/04
Ito, Robert, 7/2/31
Ives, Burl, 6/14/09
Ivory, James, 6/7/28
Ivey, Judith, 9/4/51

Jackée, 8/14/56
Jackson, Anne, 9/3/26
Jackson, Glenda, 5/9/36
Jackson, Janet, 5/16/66
Jackson, Kate, 10/29/48
Jackson, Michael, 8/29/58
Jacobi, Derek, 10/22/38
Jaffe, Sam, 3/8/1891

Jagger, Bianca, 5/2/45
Jagger, Dean, 11/7/03
Jagger, Mick, 7/26/43
Janssen, David, 3/27/30
Jarre, Maurice, 9/13/24
Jeffreys, Anne, 1/26/23
Jens, Salome, 5/8/35
Jergens, Adele, 11/27/17
Jessel, George, 4/3/1898
Jillian, Ann, 1/29/51
John, Elton, 3/25/47
Johns, Glynis, 10/5/23
Johnson, Don, 12/15/50
Johnson, Nunnally, 12/5/1897
Johnson, Laura, 8/1/27
Jones, Carolyn, 4/28/29
Jones, Dean, 1/25/35
Jones, Grace, 5/19/53
Jones, James Earl, 1/17/31
Jones, Jennifer, 3/2/19
Jones, Quincy, 3/14/33
Jones, Sam J., 8/12/54
Jones, Shirley, 3/31/34
Jones, Tom, 6/7/40
Jones, Tommy Lee, 9/15/46
Jordan, Dorothy, 8/9/08
Jordan, Richard, 7/19/38
Jory, Victor, 11/23/02
Jourdan, Louis, 6/19/19
Joy, Leatrice, 11/7/1896
Joyce, Brenda, 2/25/15
Julia, Raul, 3/9/40
Jump, Gordon, 4/1/32

Kahn, Madeline, 9/29/42
Kane, Carol, 6/18/52
Kane, Helen, 8/4/03
Kanin, Garson, 11/24/12
Karloff, Boris, 11/23/1887
Karras, Alex, 7/15/35
Katt, William, 2/16/50
Kavner, Julie, 9/7/51
Kaye, Danny, 1/18/13
Kazan, Elia, 9/7/09
Kazan, Lainie, 5/15/43
Keach, Stacy, 6/2/41
Kearns, Joanna, 2/12/53
Keaton, Buster, 10/4/1895
Keaton, Diane, 1/5/46
Keaton, Michael, 9/9/51
Keel, Howard, 4/13/17
Keeler, Ruby, 8/25/09
Keith, Brian, 11/14/21
Keith, David, 5/8/54
Kellerman, Sally, 6/2/38
Kelley, DeForest, 1/20/20
Kelly, Gene, 8/23/12
Kelly, Grace, 11/12/28
Kelly, Patsy, 1/12/10

Kelsey, Linda, 7/28/46
Kendall, Kay, 6/29/26
Kent, Barbara, 12/16/06
Kerr, Deborah, 9/30/21
Kerr, John, 11/15/31
Kilbride, Percy, 7/16/1888
Kiley, Richard, 3/31/22
Kilgallen, Dorothy, 7/3/13
King, Alan, 12/26/27
King, Perry, 4/30/48
King, Stephen, 9/21/48
Kingsley, Ben, 12/31/43
Kinski, Nastassja, 1/24/60
Kirby, Durwood, 8/24/12
Kirkland, Sally, 10/31/43
Kitt, Eartha, 1/26/30
Kline, Kevin, 10/24/47
Klugman, Jack, 4/27/22
Knight, Shirley, 7/5/37
Knight, Ted, 12/7/23
Knotts, Don, 7/21/24
Knox, Alexander, 1/16/07
Knox, Terence, 12/16/–
Kohner, Susan, 11/11/36
Korda, Sir Alexander,
  9/16/1893
Korman, Harvey, 2/15/27
Kovacs, Ernie, 1/23/19
Kramer, Stanley, 9/23/13
Kramer, Stepfanie, 8/6/56
Kreskin, 1/12/35
Kristel, Sylvia, 9/28/52
Kruger, Otto, 9/6/1885
Kubrick, Stanley, 7/26/28
Kulp, Nancy, 8/28/21
Kurosawa, Akira, 3/23/10
Kurtz, Swoosie, 9/6/44
Kwan, Nancy, 5/19/39

Ladd, Alan, 9/3/13
Ladd, Cheryl, 7/2/51
Ladd, Diane, 11/29/32
Lahr, Bert, 8/13/1895
Lahti, Christine, 4/4/50
Lake, Arthur, 4/17/05
Lake, Ricki, 9/21/68
Lake, Veronica, 11/14/19
Lamarr, Hedy, 11/9/13
Lamas, Fernando, 1/9/15
Lamas, Lorenzo, 1/20/58
Lambert, Christopher, 3/29/58
Lamour, Dorothy, 12/10/14
Lancaster, Burt, 11/2/13
Lanchester, Elsa, 10/28/02
Landau, Martin, 6/20/31
Landers, Audrey, 7/18/59
Landers, Judy, 10/7/61
Landesberg, Steve, 11/3/45
Landi, Lissa, 12/6/04

Landis, Carol, 1/1/19
Landis, Jesse Royce, 11/25/04
Lane, Lola, 5/21/09
Lane, Priscilla, 6/12/17
Lang, Fritz, 12/5/1890
Lang, June, 5/5/15
Lange, Hope, 11/28/31
Lange, Jessica, 4/20/50
Langdon, Harry, 6/15/1884
Langford, Frances, 4/4/14
Langton, Paul, 4/17/13
Lansbury, Angela, 10/16/25
Lansing, Robert, 6/5/29
La Plante, Laura, 11/1/04
La Rocque, Rod, 11/29/1896
LaRosa, Julius, 1/2/30
Larroquette, John, 11/25/47
La Rue, Al "Lash," 6/15/17
Lasser, Louise, 4/11/41
Laughton, Charles, 7/1/1899
Lauper, Cyndi, 6/20/53
Laurel, Stan, 6/16/1890
Laurie, Piper, 1/22/32
Lavin, Linda, 10/15/37
Law, John Phillip, 9/7/37
Lawford, Peter, 9/7/23
Lawrence, Carol, 9/5/34
Lawrence, Gertrude, 7/4/1898
Lawrence, Vicki, 3/26/49
Leachman, Cloris, 4/30/26
Lear, Norman, 7/27/22
Lederer, Francis, 11/6/06
Lee, Belinda, 6/15/35
Lee, Bruce, 11/27/41
Lee, Christopher, 5/27/22
Lee, Gypsy Rose, 2/9/14
Lee, Lila, 7/25/01
Lee, Michele, 6/24/42
Lee, Peggy, 5/26/20
Leibman, Ron, 10/11/37
Leigh, Janet, 7/6/27
Leigh, Vivien, 11/5/13
Leighton, Margaret, 2/26/22
Lelouch, Claude, 10/30/37
Lemmon, Chris, 1/22/54
Lemmon, Jack, 2/8/25
Leno, Jay, 4/28/51
Lenz, Kay, 3/4/53
LeRoy, Mervyn, 10/15/1900
Letterman, David, 4/12/47
Levant, Oscar, 12/27/06
Levine, Joseph E., 9/9/05
Levy, Eugene, 12/17/46
Lewis, Jerry, 3/16/26
Liberace, 5/16/19
Liberace, George, 7/31/11
Lillie, Beatrice, 5/29/1894
Lindfors, Viveca, 12/29/20
Linkletter, Art, 7/17/12

Linn-Baker, Mark, 6/17/53
Lisi, Virna, 9/8/37
Lithgow, John, 10/19/45
Little, Cleavon, 6/1/39
Little, Rich, 11/26/38
Litvak, Anatole, 5/10/02
Lloyd, Christopher, 10/22/38
Lloyd, Emily, 9/29/70
Lloyd, Harold, 4/20/1893
Lo Bianco, Tony, 10/19/38
Locke, Sondra, 5/28/47
Lockhart, June, 6/25/25
Locklear, Heather, 9/25/61
Lockwood, Gary, 2/21/37
Lockwood, Margaret, 9/15/16
Loggia, Robert, 1/3/30
Lollobrigida, Gina, 7/4/27
Lom, Herbert, 1/9/17
Lombard, Carole, 10/6/08
London, Julie, 9/26/26
Long, Richard, 12/17/27
Long, Shelley, 8/23/49
Loos, Anita, 4/26/1893
Lord, Jack, 12/30/28
Loren, Sophia, 9/20/34
Lorre, Peter, 6/26/04
Losey, Joseph, 1/14/09
Loudon, Dorothy, 9/17/30
Louise, Anita, 1/9/15
Louise, Tina, 2/11/34
Lovejoy, Frank, 3/28/14
Lovitz, John, 7/21/57
Lowe, Chad, 1/15/68
Lowe, Rob, 3/17/64
Loy, Myrna, 8/2/05
Lubitsch, Ernst, 1/28/1892
Lucci, Susan, 12/23/49
Ludden, Alan, 10/5/19
Luft, Lorna, 11/21/52
Lugosi, Bela, 10/20/1882
Lulu, 11/3/48
Lumet, Sidney, 6/25/24
Luna, Barbara, 3/2/39
Lundgren, Dolph, 10/17/59
Lundigan, William, 6/12/14
Lupino, Ida, 2/4/18
LuPone, Patti, 4/21/49
Lydon, Jimmy, 5/30/23
Lyman, Dorothy, 4/18/47
Lynde, Paul, 6/13/26
Lynley, Carol, 2/13/42
Lynn, Diana, 10/7/26
Lynn, Loretta, 4/14/35
Lyon, Sue, 7/10/46

McAvoy, May, 9/18/01
McCallum, David, 9/19/33
McCambridge, Mercedes, 3/17/18

McCarthy, Andrew, 11/29/62
McClanahan, Rue, 2/21/34
McClure, Doug, 5/11/35
McCormack, Patty, 8/21/45
McCrea, Joel, 11/5/05
McDaniel, Hattie, 6/10/1895
MacDonald, Jeanette, 6/18/01
McDowall, Roddy, 9/17/28
McDowell, Malcolm, 6/19/43
McGavin, Darren, 5/7/22
McGillis, Kelly, 7/9/57
McGoohan, Patrick, 3/19/28
McGovern, Elizabeth, 7/18/61
MacGraw, Ali, 4/1/38
McGuire, Dorothy, 6/14/18
McHattie, Stephen, 2/3/–
McIntire, John, 6/27/07
McKay, Gardner, 6/10/32
McKenna, Siobhan, 5/24/23
McKenna, Virginia, 6/7/31
MacLaine, Shirley, 4/24/34
McMahon, Ed, 3/6/23
MacMurray, Fred, 8/30/08
McNair, Barbara, 3/4/34
Macnee, Patrick, 2/6/22
McNichol, Kristy, 9/11/62
McQueen, Butterfly, 1/8/11
McQueen, Steve, 3/24/30
MacRae, Gordon, 3/12/21
McRaney, Gerald, 8/19/47
Macy, Bill, 5/18/22
Madison, Guy, 1/19/22
Madonna, 8/16/58
Magnani, Anna, 3/7/08
Maharis, George, 9/1/38
Mahoney, Jock, 2/7/19
Main, Marjorie, 2/24/1890
Majors, Lee, 4/23/42
Malden, Karl, 3/22/14
Malkovich, John, 12/9/53
Malle, Louis, 10/30/32
Mallory, Boots, 10/22/13
Malone, Dorothy, 1/30/25
Maltin, Leonard, 12/18/50
Mamoulian, Rouben, 10/8/1898
Mancini, Henry, 4/16/24
Mandel, Howie, 11/29/55
Manoff, Dianah, 1/25/58
Mansfield, Jayne, 4/19/33
Marais, Jean, 12/11/13
March, Fredric, 8/31/1897
Margolin, Janet, 7/25/43
Marin, Richard "Cheech," 7/13/46
Marinaro, Ed, 3/31/51
Marshall, E. G., 6/18/10
Marshall, Herbert, 5/23/1890
Marshall, Penny, 10/15/42

Marshall, Peter, 3/30/27
Martin, Andrea, 1/15/–
Martin, Dean, 6/17/17
Martin, Dick, 1/30/22
Martin, Jared, 12/21/44
Martin, Mary, 12/1/13
Martin, Millicent, 6/8/34
Martin, Pamela Sue, 1/5/53
Martin, Ross, 3/22/19
Martin, Steve, 8/14/45
Martin, Tony, 12/25/12
Martindale, Wink, 12/4/34
Martinez, A., 9/27/48
Marvin, Lee, 2/19/24
Marx, Chico, 3/26/1886
Marx, Groucho, 10/2/1890
Marx, Harpo, 11/21/1888
Marx, Zeppo, 2/25/01
Masina, Giulietta, 2/22/20
Mason, Jackie, 6/9/30
Mason, James, 5/15/09
Mason, Marlyn, 8/7/40
Massey, Anna, 8/11/37
Massey, Daniel, 10/10/33
Massey, Ilona, 6/16/10
Massey, Raymond, 8/30/1896
Masters, Ben, 5/6/47
Mastrantonio, M. E., 11/17/58
Mastroianni, Marcello, 9/28/23
Mathers, Jerry, 6/2/48
Matlin, Marlee, 8/24/65
Matthau, Walter, 10/1/20
Matthews, Jesse, 3/11/07
Maugham, Somerset, 1/25/1874
Maxwell, Elsa, 5/24/1883
Maxwell, Marilyn, 8/3/21
May, Elaine, 4/21/32
Mayer, Louis B., 7/4/1885
Mayo, Virginia, 11/30/20
Meadows, Audrey, 2/8/24
Meadows, Jane, 9/27/26
Meara, Anne, 9/20/29
Medford, Kay, 9/14/14
Medina, Patricia, 7/19/20
Meeker, Ralph, 11/21/20
Menjou, Aldophe, 2/18/1890
Merchant, Ismael, 12/25/36
Mercouri, Melina, 10/18/23
Meredith, Don, 4/10/38
Meredith, Burgess, 11/16/08
Meriwether, Lee, 5/27/35
Merkel, Una, 12/10/03
Merman, Ethel, 1/16/09
Messel, Oliver, 1/13/04
Meyers, Russ, 3/21/23
Midler, Bette, 12/1/45
Miles, Sarah, 12/31/41

Miles, Sylvia, 9/9/32
Miles, Vera, 8/23/29
Milland, Ray, 1/3/05
Miller, Ann, 4/12/19
Miller, Denny (Scott), 4/25/34
Miller, Henry, 12/26/1891
Miller, Jason, 4/22/39
Miller, Roger, 1/2/36
Mills, Donna, 12/11/43
Mills, Hayley, 4/18/46
Mills, John, 2/22/08
Milner, Martin, 12/28/27
Mimieux, Yvette, 1/8/39
Mineo, Sal, 1/10/39
Minnelli, Liza, 3/12/46
Minnelli, Vincente, 2/28/10
Miranda, Carmen, 2/9/09
Miranda, Isa, 7/5/09
Mitchum, Robert, 8/6/17
Modine, Matthew, 3/22/60
Monroe, Marilyn, 6/1/26
Montalban, Ricardo, 11/25/20
Montand, Yves, 10/13/21
Montez, Maria, 6/6/20
Montgomery, Elizabeth, 4/15/33
Montgomery, Robert, 5/21/04
Moore, Clayton, 9/14/14
Moore, Constance, 1/18/19
Moore, Demi, 11/11/62
Moore, Dudley, 4/19/35
Moore, Grace, 12/5/01
Moore, Mary Tyler, 12/29/36
Moore, Roger, 10/14/28
Moore, Terry, 1/7/29
Moorehead, Agnes, 12/6/06
Moorhead, Natalie, 7/27/–
Moranis, Rick, 4/18/54
Moreau, Jean, 1/23/28
Moreno, Rita, 12/11/31
Morgan, Dennis, 12/10/10
Morgan, Harry, 4/10/15
Morgan, Henry, 3/31/15
Morgan, Michèle, 2/29/20
Moriarty, Michael, 4/5/41
Morley, Robert, 5/25/08
Morris, Chester, 2/16/01
Morris, Garrett, 2/1/37
Morris, Howard, 9/4/19
Morse, David, 10/11/53
Morse, Robert, 5/18/31
Moses, William R., 11/17/59
Mostel, Zero, 2/28/15
Mostel, Joshua, 12/21/57
Moyers, Bill, 6/5/34
Muldaur, Diana, 8/19/43
Mulgrew, Kate, 4/29/55
Mullavey, Greg, 9/10/39
Mulligan, Richard, 11/13/32

Muni, Paul, 9/22/1895
Munsel, Patrice, 5/14/25
Murphy, Eddie, 4/3/61
Murray, Bill, 9/21/50
Murray, Don, 7/31/29
Murray, Jan, 10/4/17
Murrow, Edward R., 4/25/08
Music, Lorenzo, 5/2/37

Nabors, Jim, 6/12/32
Nader, George, 10/19/21
Nagel, Conrad, 3/16/1897
Natwick, Mildred, 6/19/08
Naughton, David, 2/13/51
Naughton, James, 12/6/45
Nazimova, Alla, 6/4/1879
Neagle, Dame Anna, 10/20/04
Neal, Patricia, 1/20/26
Neff, Hildegarde, 12/28/25
Negri, Pola, 12/31/1894
Negron, Taylor, 8/1/–
Nelligan, Kate, 3/16/51
Nelson, Craig T., 4/4/46
Nelson, David, 10/24/36
Nelson, Harriet, 7/18/14
Nelson, Judd, 11/28/59
Nelson, Ozzie, 3/20/07
Nelson, Rick, 5/8/40
Nesbitt, Cathleen, 11/24/1888
Newhart, Bob, 9/5/29
Newley, Anthony, 9/24/31
Newman, Laraine, 3/2/52
Newman, Paul, 1/26/25
Newman, Phyllis, 3/19/35
Newmar, Julie, 8/16/35
Newton-John, Olivia, 9/26/48
Newton, Wayne, 4/3/42
Nichols, Barbara, 12/30/29
Nichols, Mike, 11/6/31
Nicholson, Jack, 4/22/37
Nielsen, Brigitte, 5/17/63
Nielson, Leslie, 2/11/26
Nimoy, Leonard, 3/26/31
Niven, David, 3/1/09
Nolan, Lloyd, 8/11/02
Nolte, Nick, 2/8/41
Normand, Mabel, 11/16/1894
Norris, Chuck, 3/10/42
North, Jay, 8/3/52
North, Sheree, 1/17/33
Novak, Kim, 2/13/33
Novello, Ivor, 1/15/1893
Nuyen, France, 7/31/39
Nye, Louis, 5/1/–

Oates, Warren, 7/5/28
Oberon, Merle, 2/19/11
O'Brian, Hugh, 4/19/25
O'Brien, Edmond, 9/10/15

O'Brien, Margaret, 1/15/37
O'Brien, Virginia, 4/18/21
O'Connor, Carroll, 8/2/25
O'Connor, Donald, 8/28/25
O'Connor, Glynnis, 11/19/55
O'Connor, Una, 10/23/1880
O'Driscoll, Martha, 3/4/22
O'Hara, Maureen, 8/17/20
Oland, Warner, 10/3/1880
Oldman, Gary, 3/21/59
Olin, Ken, 7/30/54
Oliver, Edna May, 11/9/1883
Olivier, Lord Laurence, 5/22/07
Olmos, Edward James, 2/24/47
Olson, Nancy, 7/14/28
O'Neal, Patrick, 9/26/27
O'Neal, Ryan, 4/20/41
O'Neal, Tatum, 11/5/63
O'Neill, Ed, 4/12/–
O'Neill, Jennifer, 2/20/48
Ontkean, Michael, 1/24/46
Opuls (Ophüls), Max, 5/6/02
Orry-Kelly, 12/31/1897
O'Shea, Tessie, 3/13/17
Osmond, Ken, 6/7/–
O'Toole, Annette, 4/1/52
O'Toole, Peter, 8/2/32
Oxenberg, Catherine, 9/22/61
Oz, Frank, 5/25/44

Paar, Jack, 5/1/18
Pacino, Al, 4/25/40
Page, Anita, 8/4/10
Page, Geraldine, 11/22/24
Page, Patti, 11/8/27
Paige, Janis, 9/16/22
Palance, Jack, 2/18/19
Paulette, Eugene, 7/8/1889
Palmer, Betsy, 11/1/29
Palmer, Lilli, 5/24/14
Papas, Irene, 3/9/26
Pardo, Don, 2/22/–
Paré, Michael, 10/9/59
Parker, Cecilia, 4/26/05
Parker, Dorothy, 8/22/1893
Parker, Eleanor, 6/26/22
Parker, Jameson, 11/18/47
Parker, Suzy, 10/28/33
Parkins, Barbara, 5/22/42
Parks, Bert, 12/30/14
Parks, Michael, 4/4/38
Parrish, Helen, 3/12/22
Parsons, Estelle, 11/20/27
Parsons, Louella, 8/6/1893
Parton, Dolly, 1/19/46
Pascal, Jean-Claude, 10/24/27
Patrick, Butch, 6/2/–

Patton, Will, 6/14/54
Payne, John, 5/23/12
Pearl, Minnie, 10/25/12
Pearlman, Rhea, 3/31/48
Pearson, Drew, 12/13/1897
Peck, Gregory, 4/5/16
Peckinpah, Sam, 2/21/25
Penn, Sean, 8/17/60
Penny, Joe, 9/14/56
Peppard, George, 10/1/28
Perkins, Anthony, 4/14/32
Perkins, Elizabeth, 11/18/60
Perrine, Valerie, 9/3/44
Perry, L. T. "Stepin Fetchit," 5/30/02
Perry, Luke, 10/11/65
Pesci, Joe, 2/9/43
Peters, Bernadette, 2/28/48
Petersen, Paul, 9/23/45
Pettet, Joanna, 11/16/44
Pfeiffer, Michelle, 4/29/57
Pflug, Jo Ann, 5/2/–
Phillips, Lou Diamond, 2/17/62
Phillips, Michelle, 4/6/44
Phoenix, River, 8/23/70
Pickens, Slim, 6/29/19
Pickford, Mary, 4/8/1893
Pidgeon, Walter, 9/23/1897
Pinchot, Bronson, 5/20/59
Piscopo, Joe, 6/17/51
Pisier, Marie-France, 5/10/44
Pitts, Zasu, 1/3/1898
Place, Mary Kay, 9/23/47
Plato, Dana, 11/7/64
Pleasance, Donald, 10/5/19
Pleshette, John, 7/27/42
Pleshette, Suzanne, 1/31/37
Plimpton, Martha, 11/16/70
Plowright, Joan, 10/28/29
Plumb, Eve, 4/29/57
Plummer, Amanda, 3/23/57
Plummer, Christopher, 12/13/27
Plunkett, Walter, 6/5/02
Pointer, Priscilla, 5/18/–
Poitier, Sidney, 2/20/24
Polanski, Roman, 8/17/33
Pollan, Tracy, 6/22/62
Pollard, Michael J., 5/30/39
Ponti, Carlo, 12/11/10
Porizkova, Paulina, 4/9/65
Porter, Cole, 6/9/1892
Powell, Dick, 11/14/04
Powell, Jane, 4/1/29
Powell, William, 7/29/1892
Power, Tyrone, Sr., 5/2/1869
Power, Tyrone, 5/5/13
Powers, Stefanie, 10/12/42

Preminger, Otto, 12/5/06
Prentiss, Paula, 3/4/39
Presley, Elvis, 1/8/35
Presley, Priscilla, 5/24/45
Presnell, Harve, 9/14/33
Preston, Robert, 6/8/18
Price, Vincent, 5/27/11
Priestly, Jason, 8/29/69
Prince, 6/7/58
Prinze, Freddie, 6/22/54
Provine, Dorothy, 1/20/37
Prowse, Juliet, 9/25/36
Pryor, Richard, 12/1/40
Purdom, Edward, 12/19/24
Purl, Linda, 9/2/55

Quaid, Dennis, 4/9/54
Quaid, Randy, 10/1/50
Quayle, Anthony, 9/7/13
Quinn, Aidan, 3/8/59
Quinn, Anthony, 4/21/15

Rachins, Alan, 10/10/–
Radner, Gilda, 6/28/46
Rae, Charlotte, 4/22/26
Raffin, Deborah, 3/13/53
Raft, George, 9/26/1895
Rainer, Louise, 1/12/10
Rains, Claude, 11/10/1889
Ralston, Vera Hruba, 6/12/21
Ramis, Harold, 11/21/44
Rambova, Natacha, 1/19/1897
Rampling, Charlotte, 2/5/45
Rand, Ayn, 2/2/05
Randall, Tony, 2/26/20
Randolph, Joyce, 10/21/25
Rappaport, David, 11/23/52
Rashad, Phylicia, 6/17/48
Rathbone, Basil, 6/13/1892
Rattigan, Sir Terence, 6/10/11
Ratzenberger, John, 4/6/47
Ray, Aldo, 9/25/26
Raye, Martha, 8/27/16
Raymond, Gene, 8/13/08
Reagan, Nancy (Davis), 7/6/21
Reagan, Ronald, 2/6/11
Redford, Robert, 8/18/37
Redgrave, Lynn, 3/8/43
Redgrave, Vanessa, 1/30/37
Reed, Donna, 1/27/21
Reed, Oliver, 2/13/38
Reed, Pamela, 4/2/49
Reed, Rex, 10/2/39
Reed, Robert, 10/19/32
Reese, Della, 7/6/32
Reeve, Christopher, 9/25/52
Reeves, George, 4/6/14
Reeves, Keanu, 9/2/65
Reeves, Steve, 1/21/26

Reid, Beryl, 6/17/20
Reid, Kate, 11/4/30
Reid, Tim, 12/19/44
Reilly, Charles Nelson, 1/13/31
Reiner, Carl, 3/20/22
Reiner, Rob, 3/6/47
Reiser, Paul, 3/30/57
Remick, Lee, 12/14/35
Rennie, Michael, 8/25/09
Rey, Fernando, 9/20/15
Reynolds, Burt, 2/11/36
Reynolds, Debbie, 4/1/32
Rhue, Madlyn, 10/3/34
Rich, Buddy, 6/30/17
Richardson, Natasha, 5/11/64
Richardson, Sir Ralph, 12/19/02
Rickles, Don, 5/8/26
Rigg, Diana, 7/20/38
Ringwald, Molly, 2/18/68
Ritter, John, 9/17/48
Ritter, Tex, 1/12/05
Ritter, Thelma, 2/14/05
Rivera, Geraldo, 7/4/43
Rivers, Joan, 6/8/35
Robards, Jason, Jr., 7/22/22
Robbins, Tim, 10/16/58
Roberti, Lyda, 5/20/06
Roberts, Beverly, 5/19/14
Roberts, Eric, 4/18/56
Roberts, Julia, 10/28/67
Roberts, Pernell, 5/18/28
Roberts, Rachel, 9/20/27
Roberts, Tanya, 10/15/55
Robertson, Cliff, 9/9/25
Robeson, Paul, 4/9/1898
Robinson, Bill "Bojangles," 5/26/1878
Robinson, Edward G., 12/12/1893
Robson, Dame Flora, 3/28/02
Robson, May, 4/19/1858
Rocco, Alex, 2/29/36
Rogers, Charles "Buddy," 8/13/04
Rogers, Ginger, 7/16/11
Rogers, Roy, 11/5/12
Rogers, Wayne, 4/7/33
Rogers, Will, 11/4/1879
Rolle, Esther, 11/8/22
Roman, Ruth, 12/22/24
Romero, Cesar, 2/15/07
Rooney, Mickey, 9/23/20
Rose, Billy, 9/6/1899
Rose, David, 6/15/10
Rose Marie, 8/15/23
Ross, Diana, 3/26/44
Ross, Katharine, 1/29/42
Ross, Shirley, 1/7/09

Rossellini, Isabella, 6/18/52
Rossellini, Roberto, 5/8/06
Roth, Lillian, 12/13/10
Roundtree, Richard, 7/9/42
Rowan, Dan, 7/2/22
Rowlands, Gena, 6/19/34
Rubinstein, John, 12/8/46
Rule, Janice, 8/15/31
Runyon, Damon, 10/8/–
Rush, Barbara, 1/4/27
Russell, Jane, 6/21/21
Russell, Ken, 7/3/27
Russell, Kurt, 3/17/51
Russell, Rosalind, 6/4/08
Russell, Theresa, 3/20/57
Rutherford, Ann, 11/2/17
Rutherford, Dame Margaret, 5/11/1892
Ryan, Irene, 10/17/03
Ryan, Meg, 11/19/62
Ryan, Robert, 11/11/09
Rydell, Bobby, 4/26/42
Ryder, Winona, 10/29/71

Sabu, 1/27/24
Saint, Eva Marie, 7/4/24
Saint James, Susan, 8/14/46
St. John, Jill, 8/19/40
Sajak, Pat, 10/26/47
Sale, Richard, 12/17/11
Sales, John, 9/28/49
Sales, Soupy, 1/8/26
Samms, Emma, 8/28/61
Sanders, George, 7/3/06
Sanford, Isabel, 8/29/17
Santiago, Saundra, 4/13/57
Sarandon, Chris, 7/24/42
Sarandon, Susan, 10/4/46
Saroyan, William, 8/31/08
Sarrazin, Michael, 5/22/40
Savalas, George, 12/5/26
Savalas, Telly, 1/21/25
Saxon, John, 8/5/35
Scalia, Jack, 11/10/51
Scarwid, Diana, 8/27/55
Schary, Dory, 8/31/05
Scheider, Roy, 11/10/35
Schell, Maria, 1/5/26
Schell, Maximilian, 12/8/30
Schenck, Joseph, 12/25/1878
Schneider, John, 4/8/54
Schneider, Romy, 9/23/38
Schroder, Rick, 4/13/70
Schwarzenegger, Arnold, 7/30/47
Scofield, Paul, 1/21/22
Scolari, Peter, 9/12/54
Scorsesse, Martin, 11/17/42
Scott, George C., 10/18/27

Scott, Lizabeth, 9/29/22
Scott, Randolph, 1/23/03
Scott, Zachary, 2/24/14
Seberg, Jean, 11/13/38
Segal, George, 2/13/34
Segal, Vivienne, 4/19/1897
Seidlman, Susan, 12/11/52
Selby, David, 2/5/41
Sellecca, Connie, 5/25/55
Selleck, Tom, 1/29/45
Sellers, Peter, 9/8/25
Selznick, David O., 5/10/02
Sennett, Mack, 1/17/1880
Serling, Rod, 12/25/24
Severinsen, Doc, 7/7/27
Seymour, Jane, 2/15/51
Shackelford, Ted, 6/23/46
Shafer, Natalie, 11/5/12
Shaffer, Paul, 11/28/49
Shane, Maxwell, 8/26/05
Sharif, Omar, 4/10/32
Shatner, William, 3/22/31
Shaw, Irwin, 2/27/13
Shaw, Robert, 8/9/27
Shaw, Winifred "Wini," 2/25/1899
Shawn, Dick, 12/1/29
Shearer, Moira, 1/26/26
Shearer, Norma, 8/10/1900
Sheedy, Ally, 6/13/62
Sheen, Charlie, 9/3/65
Sheen, Martin, 8/3/40
Sheldon, Sidney, 2/11/17
Shepard, Sam, 11/5/43
Shepherd, Cybill, 2/18/50
Sheridan, Ann, 2/21/15
Sheridan, Nicollette, 11/21/–
Sherwood, Madeleine, 11/13/26
Shields, Brooke, 5/31/65
Shire, Talia, 4/25/47
Shore, Dinah, 3/1/17
Short, Martin, 3/26/50
Shriver, Maria, 11/6/55
Sidney, Sylvia, 8/8/10
Signoret, Simone, 3/25/21
Silver, Ron, 7/2/46
Silverheels, Jay "Tonto," 5/26/19
Silvers, Phil, 5/11/12
Simmons, Jean, 1/31/29
Simon, Neil, 7/4/27
Sim, Alastair, 10/9/1900
Sinatra, Frank, 12/12/15
Singer, Lori, 5/6/62
Singer, Marc, 1/29/48
Singleton, Penny, 9/15/08
Skelton, Red, 7/18/13
Skerritt, Tom, 8/25/33

Slater, Christian, 8/18/69
Slater, Helen, 12/15/65
Slezak, Walter, 5/3/20
Sloane, Everett, 10/1/09
Smith, Alexis, 6/8/21
Smith, C. Aubrey, 7/21/1863
Smith, Jaclyn, 10/26/47
Smith, Kate, 5/1/07
Smith, Kent, 3/19/07
Smith, Liz, 2/2/23
Smith, Dame Maggie, 12/28/34
Smith, Roger, 12/18/32
Smits, Jimmy, 7/9/58
Snodgress, Carrie, 10/27/46
Somers, Suzanne, 10/16/46
Sommer, Elke, 11/5/40
Sondergaard, 2/15/1899
Sothern, Ann, 1/22/09
Soul, David, 8/28/43
Spacek, Sissy, 12/25/49
Spacey, Kevin, 7/26/59
Spader, James, 2/7/60
Spelling, Tori, 5/16/73
Spielberg, Steven, 12/18/47
Spillane, Mickey, 3/9/18
Stack, Robert, 1/13/19
Stallone, Sylvester, 7/6/46
Stamos, John, 8/19/63
Stamp, Terence, 7/23/40
Stander, Lionel, 1/11/08
Stanley, Kim, 2/11/25
Stanton, Harry Dean, 7/14/26
Stanwyck, Barbara, 7/16/07
Stapleton, Jean, 1/19/23
Stapleton, Maureen, 6/21/25
Steele, Barbara, 12/29/38
Steele, Tommy, 12/17/36
Steiger, Rod, 4/14/25
Steiner, Max, 5/10/1888
Sterling, Jan, 4/3/23
Sternberg, Josef von, 5/29/1894
Stevens, Andrew, 6/10/55
Stevens, Connie, 8/8/38
Stevens, Craig, 7/8/18
Stevens, Fisher, 11/27/63
Stevens, George, 12/18/04
Stevens, Inger, 10/18/34
Stevens, Stella, 10/1/36
Stevenson, Parker, 6/4/52
Stewart, James, 5/20/08
Stiers, David Ogden, 10/31/42
Sting, 10/2/51
Stockwell, Dean, 3/5/36
Stockwell, Guy, 11/16/33
Stoller, Shirley, 3/30/29
Stone, Dee Wallace, 12/14/–
Stone, Louis, 11/15/1879

Stone, Oliver, 9/15/46
Straight, Beatrice, 8/2/18
Strasberg, Lee, 11/17/01
Strasberg, Susan, 5/22/38
Stratten, Dorothy, 2/28/–
Strauss, Peter, 2/20/47
Streep, Meryl, 6/22/51
Streisand, Barbra, 4/24/42
Stroheim, Erich von, 9/22/1885
Struthers, Sally, 7/28/47
Sullavan, Margaret, 5/16/11
Sullivan, Ed, 9/28/01
Sumac, Yuma, 9/10/22
Susann, Jacqueline, 8/20/21
Susskind, David, 12/19/20
Sutherland, Donald, 7/17/34
Sutherland, Keifer, 12/21/67
Suzman, Janet, 2/9/39
Swanson, Gloria, 3/27/1897
Swayze, Patrick, 8/18/54
Sweet, Blanche, 6/18/1895
Swenson, Inga, 12/29/32
Swit, Loretta, 11/4/37
Switzer, Carl "Alfalfa," 8/8/26
Sydow, Max von, 4/10/29
Syms, Sylvia, 1/6/34

T, Mr. (Lawrence Tero), 5/21/52
Tabori, Kristoffer, 8/4/55
Takei, George, 4/20/40
Tamlyn, Russ, 12/30/34
Tandy, Jessica, 6/7/09
Taylor, Buck, 5/13/38
Taylor, Elizabeth, 2/27/32
Taylor, Rip, 1/13/34
Taylor, Robert, 8/5/11
Taylor, Rod, 1/11/29
Taylor, William Desmond, 4/26/1877
Taylor-Young, Leigh, 1/25/44
Temple, Shirley, 4/23/28
Tennant, Victoria, 9/30/53
Terry, Philip, 3/7/09
Terry, Ruth, 10/21/20
Tesh, John, 7/9/52
Terry-Thomas, 7/14/11
Thalberg, Irving, 5/30/1899
Thigpen, Lynne, 12/22/–
Thinnes, Roy, 4/6/38
Thomas, Danny, 1/6/14
Thomas, Dave, 5/20/–
Thomas, Marlo, 11/21/37
Thomas, Richard, 6/13/51
Thomas, William, "Buckwheat," 3/12/31
Thompson, Sada, 9/27/29
Thorndike, Dame Sybil,

10/24/1882
Thorson, Linda, 6/18/47
Thulin, Ingrid, 1/27/29
Thurman, Uma, 4/29/70
Tierney, Gene, 11/20/20
Tiffin, Pamela, 11/13/42
Tilly, Meg, 2/14/60
Tilton, Charlene, 12/1/58
Todd, Ann, 1/24/09
Todd, Mike, 6/22/07
Todd, Richard, 6/11/19
Todd, Thelma, 7/29/05
Tognazzi, Ugo, 3/23/22
Tomlin, Lily, 9/1/39
Tone, Franchot, 2/27/05
Topol, 9/9/35
Torme, Mel, 9/13/25
Torn, Rip, 2/6/31
Totter, Audrey, 12/20/18
Townsend, Robert, 2/6/66
Tracy, Lee, 4/14/1898
Tracy, Spencer, 4/5/1900
Travanti, Daniel J., 3/7/40
Travolta, John, 2/18/54
Treacher, Arthur, 7/23/1894
Trebek, Alex, 7/22/40
Trevor, Claire, 4/8/09
Tucker, Forrest, 2/12/19
Tucker, Lorenzo "The Black Valentino," 6/27/1900
Turner, Janine, 12/6/62
Turner, Kathleen, 6/19/54
Turner, Lana, 2/8/20
Turner, Ted, 11/19/38
Turner, Tina, 11/26/38
Tushingham, Rita, 3/14/42
Tweed, Shannon, 3/10/–
Twelvetrees, Helen, 12/25/07
Twiggy, 9/19/49
Tyson, Cecily, 12/19/32

Ullman, Tracey, 12/30/59
Ullmann, Liv, 12/16/39
Urich, Robert, 12/19/46
Ustinov, Peter, 4/16/21

Vaccaro, Brenda, 11/18/39
Vadim, Roger, 1/26/28
Valente, Caterina, 1/14/31
Valentine, Karen, 5/25/47
Valentino, Rudolph, 5/6/1895
Vallee, Rudy, 7/28/01
Vallone, Raf, 2/17/17
Van Ark, Joan, 6/16/43
Vance, Vivian, 7/26/11
Van Cleef, Lee, 1/9/25
Van Damme, Jean-Claude, 10/18/61
Van Devere, Trish, 3/9/45

Van Doren, Mamie, 2/6/31
Van Dyke, Dick, 12/13/25
Van Dyke, Jerry, 7/27/31
Van Fleet, Jo, 12/30/19
Van Patten, Joyce, 3/9/34
Van Peebles, Melvin, 8/21/32
Varsi, Diane, 2/23/37
Vaughn, Robert, 11/30/32
Velez, Lupe, 7/18/08
Vera-Ellen, 2/17/26
Verdon, Gwen, 1/13/25
Verdugo, Elena, 4/20/26
Vereen, Ben, 10/10/46
Vidal, Gore, 10/3/25
Vigoda, Abe, 2/24/21
Vincent, Jan-Michael, 7/15/44
Visconti, Luchino, 11/2/06
Vitti, Monica, 11/3/31
Voight, Jon, 12/29/38

Wahl, Ken, 2/14/53
Waggoner, Lyle, 4/13/35
Wagner, Lindsay, 6/22/49
Wagner, Robert, 2/10/30
Walken, Christopher, 3/31/43
Walker, Clint, 5/30/27
Walker, Nancy, 5/10/21
Walker, Robert, 10/13/18
Wallace, Jean, 10/12/23
Wallach, Eli, 12/7/15
Walley, Deborah, 8/12/43
Walsh, M. Emmet, 3/22/35
Walston, Ray, 11/22/18
Walter, Jessica, 1/31/40
Walters, Barbara, 9/25/31
Wanger, Walter, 7/11/1894
Ward, Fred, 12/30/43
Ward, Simon, 10/19/41
Warden, Jack, 9/18/20
Warhol, Andy, 8/6/27
Warner, David, 7/29/41
Warren, Lesley Ann, 8/16/46
Warrick, Dionne, 12/12/41
Warrick, Ruth, 6/29/15
Washbourne, Mona, 11/27/03
Washington, Denzel, 12/28/54
Wasson, Craig, 3/15/54
Waters, Ethel, 10/31/1896
Waterston, Sam, 11/15/40
Watson, Lucille, 5/27/1879
Wayne, David, 1/30/14
Wayne, John, 5/26/07
Wayne, Patrick, 7/15/39
Weathers, Carl, 1/14/48
Weaver, Dennis, 6/4/24
Weaver, Fritz, 1/19/26
Weaver, Sigourney, 10/8/49
Webb, Clifton, 11/19/1891
Webb, Jack, 4/2/20

Webber, Robert, 10/14/24
Wedgeworth, Ann, 1/21/35
Weir, Peter, 8/21/44
Weissmuller, Johnny, 6/2/04
Welch, Raquel, 9/5/40
Weld, Tuesday, 8/27/43
Welk, Lawrence, 3/11/03
Weller, Peter, 6/24/47
Welles, Orson, 5/6/15
Wellman, William, 2/29/1896
Werner, Oskar, 11/13/22
Wertmuller, Lena, 8/14/28
West, Adam, 9/19/28
West, Mae, 8/17/1892
Westheimer, Dr. Ruth, 6/4/28
Wheaton, Wil, 7/29/72
White, Betty, 1/17/22
White, Jaleel, 11/27/76
Whitman, Stuart, 2/1/26
Whitty, Dame Mae, 6/19/1865
Widmark, Richard, 12/26/14
Wiest, Dianne, 3/28/48
Wilcox, Robert, 5/19/10
Wilcoxon, Henry, 9/8/05

Wilde, Cornel, 10/13/15
Wilder, Billy, 6/22/06
Wilder, Gene, 6/11/35
Wilding, Michael, 7/23/12
William, Warren, 12/2/1895
Williams, Billy Dee, 4/6/37
Williams, Cindy, 8/22/47
Williams, Clarence III,
    8/21/39
Williams, Emlyn, 11/26/05
Williams, Esther, 8/8/23
Williams, Grant, 8/18/30
Williams, Robin, 7/21/52
Williams, Treat, 12/1/51
Williams, Vanessa, 3/18/63
Williamson, Nicol, 9/14/38
Willis, Bruce, 3/19/55
Wilson, Earl, 5/3/07
Wilson, Flip, 12/8/33
Wilson, Lois, 6/28/1896
Wilson, Marie, 8/19/16
Winchell, Walter, 4/7/1897
Windom, William, 9/28/23
Windsor, Marie, 12/11/22

Winfield, Paul, 5/22/41
Winfrey, Oprah, 1/29/54
Wing, Toby, 7/14/13
Winger, Debra, 5/17/55
Winkler, Henry, 10/30/45
Winningham, Mare, 5/6/59
Winslow, George "Foghorn,"
    5/3/46
Winters, Jonathan, 11/11/25
Winters, Shelley, 8/18/22
Winwood, Estelle, 1/24/1883
Withers, Googie, 3/12/17
Withers, Jane, 4/12/26
Wong, Anna May, 1/3/07
Wood, Natalie, 7/20/38
Woodard, Alfre, 11/8/53
Woods, James, 4/18/47
Woodward, Edward, 6/1/30
Woodward, Joanne, 2/27/30
Woolley, Monte, 8/17/1888
Worth, Irene, 6/23/16
Wray, Fay, 9/15/07
Wyatt, Jane, 8/12/12
Wyler, Gretchen, 2/16/32

Wyman, Jane, 1/4/14
Wynard, Diana, 1/16/06
Wynette, Tammy, 5/4/42
Wynn, Ed, 11/9/1886
Wynn, Keenan, 7/27/16
Wynter, Dana, 6/8/30

York, Dick, 9/4/28
York, Michael, 3/27/42
York, Susannah, 1/9/41
Young, Gig, 11/4/13
Young, Loretta, 1/6/13
Young, Robert, 2/22/07
Young, Roland, 11/11/1887
Young, Sean, 11/20/60
Youngman, Henny, 1/12/06

Zanuck, Darryl F., 9/5/02
Zeffirelli, Franco, 2/12/23
Zimbalist, Efrem, Jr., 11/30/18
Zimbalist, Stephanie, 10/6/56
Zorina, Vera, 1/2/17
Zucco, George, 1/11/1886

PHOTOGRAPH ACKNOWLEDGMENTS & COPYRIGHTS

The majority of the photographs in this book are courtesy of Turner Entertainment Co., Los Angeles; Warner Bros. Collection at the University of Southern California School of Cinema-Television; Margaret Herrick Library, Academy of Motion Picture Arts and Sciences; Warner Bros. Collection at George Eastman House.

With the exception of *Laura* (listed below) and Victor Fleming's party on the set of *The Wizard of Oz*, courtesy of James Kotsilibas Davis, all photographs used on the covers, endsheets, and in the Introduction are from the MGM Collection.

Additional copyright information for photographs facing the "listing" pages are given below in alphabetical order by film title:
The Bride of Frankenstein, Copyright © by Universal City Studios, Inc. Courtesy of MCA Publishing Rights, a Division of MCA Inc. Elsa Lanchester's image used courtesy of the Motion Picture and Television Fund.
Gilda, Copyright 1946, Renewed 1973 Columbia Pictures Industries, Inc. All Rights Reserved. Courtesy of Columbia Pictures.
Golden Boy, Copyright 1939, Renewed 1967 Columbia Pictures Industries, Inc. All Rights Reserved. Courtesy of Columbia Pictures.
Go West Young Man, Copyright © by Universal City Studios, Inc. Courtesy of MCA Publishing Rights, a Division of MCA Inc.
King of the Jungle, Copyright © by Universal City Studios, Inc. Courtesy of MCA Publishing Rights, a Division of MCA Inc.
Laura, © 1944 Twentieth Century-Fox Corporation. All Rights Reserved.
My Cousin Rachel, © 1953 Twentieth Century-Fox Corporation. All Rights Reserved.
Sabrina, Copyright © 1993 by Paramount Pictures. All Rights Reserved. Courtesy of Paramount Pictures.
Shanghai Express, Copyright © by Universal City Studios, Inc. Courtesy of MCA Publishing Rights, a Division of MCA Inc.

Thanks go to Stuart Ng of the Warner Bros. Collection at the University of Southern California School of Cinema-Television; Robert Cushman and Dan Woodruff of the Margaret Herrick Library, Academy of Motion Picture Arts and Sciences; Christopher Horack of George Eastman House; and Producers Photo Lab, Hollywood.
Front cover photograph of Jean Harlow is by George Hurrell for MGM, rephotographed for the cover by Tina Mucci.

In clearing photographic permissions, the publisher has made every diligent effort to locate the heirs or estate of all persons included in this volume.